Contents

Detailed Contents

As per NCF 2023

OXFORD

LEARNER'S GRAMMAR AND COMPOSITION

Middle Stage

6

Sanghita Sen

OXFORD
UNIVERSITY PRESS

OXFORD
UNIVERSITY PRESS

Oxford University Press is a department of the University of Oxford. It furthers the University's objective of excellence in research, scholarship, and education by publishing worldwide. Oxford is a registered trade mark of Oxford University Press in the UK and in certain other countries.

Published in India by
Oxford University Press
22 Workspace, 2nd Floor, 1/22 Asaf Ali Road, New Delhi 110002, India

First Edition published in 2010
Second Edition published in 2018
This New Edition published in 2025

ISBN-13: 9789361032042
Typeset in Calibri
by AnIdeaz Media International Pvt. Ltd., New Delhi 110015
Printed in India by Manipal Technologies Limited

Illustrations by AnIdeaz Media International Pvt. Ltd., New Delhi 110015
Cover Illustration by Weaverbird Interactive, New Delhi 110088

Introduction

Oxford Learner's Grammar and Composition is a series of eight books aligned to the National Curriculum Framework 2023 that introduces learners to the basics of English language. The books are well graded, focusing on structural as well as functional grammar. With contextualized examples, detailed explanations and ample exercises, the books aim to build a strong foundation in grammar. Assessments in the books are designed to achieve the learning outcomes and the competencies outlined in NCF 2023. Taking the vision of NEP 2020 and NCF 2023 forward, the books provide a holistic learning experience by equipping the learners with 21st century skills.

New Features

- NEP and NCF aligned with a holistic learning experience
- Cloze passages that help to assess the students' vocabulary, spelling and language skills all at the same time
- Exercises aiding listening and speaking skills
- Multi-disciplinary learning through cross-curricular exercises
- Activities based on art integration and experiential learning that build 21st century skills
- Test papers with periodic self assessment checks to aid competency-based learning

New improved **Teacher's Handbooks** that include:

- a teacher's copy with worked out exercises from the book
- tags to indicate Bloom's Taxonomy
- extensive worksheets
- additional activities
- notes and tips

Let's Practise

1. Some action words are given below. Change them into abstract nouns.

a. see	sight	g. prevent	prevention
b. attract	attraction	h. injure	injury
c. discuss	discussion	i. console	consolation
d. argue	argument	j. assist	assistance
e. agree	agreement	k. attach	attachment
f. locate	location	l. approve	approval

Introducing **digital learning** on Oxford Educate the digital companion to the books with:

- interactive ebooks
- games
- interactivities
- audio-visual explainers

To access these assets, go to www.oxfordeducate.in or scan

Learning Path

1

Let's Do

Coo Boo is a little calf. Read what he has to say.

I am Coo Boo. This is my mother. This is the shed where we live. Those are the other cows. I like the black calf there. He is my friend. We are always

Let's Do: Stimulating exercises that check previous learning as well as introduce new rules

2

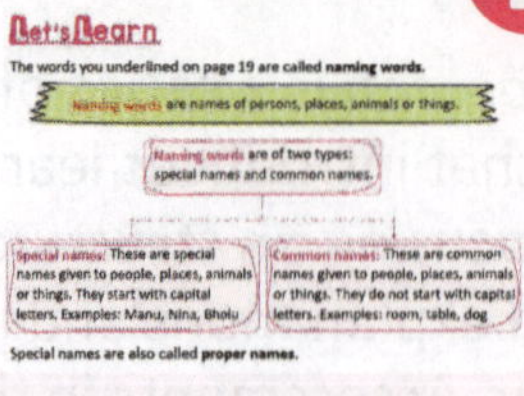

Let's Learn

The words you underlined on page 19 are called naming words.

Naming words are names of persons, places, animals or things.

Naming words are of two types: special names and common names.

Special names: These are special names given to people, places, animals or things. They start with capital letters. Examples: Manu, Nina, Bholu

Common names: These are common names given to people, places, animals or things. They do not start with capital letters. Examples: room, table, dog

Special names are also called proper names.

Let's Learn: Detailed explanations, definitions and examples of the grammar topics

3

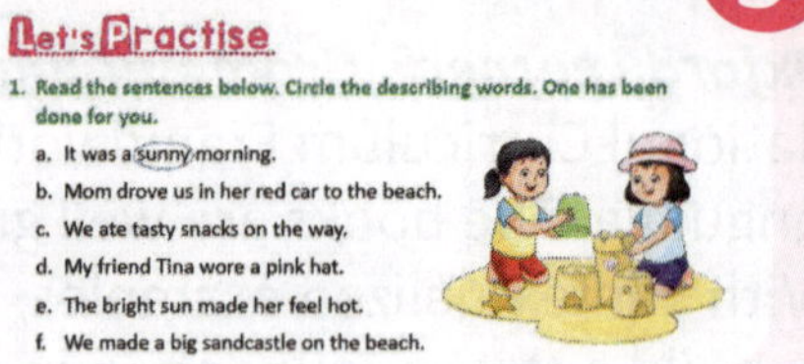

Let's Practise

1. Read the sentences below. Circle the describing words. One has been done for you.
   a. It was a sunny morning.
   b. Mom drove us in her red car to the beach.
   c. We ate tasty snacks on the way.
   d. My friend Tina wore a pink hat.
   e. The bright sun made her feel hot.
   f. We made a big sandcastle on the beach.

Let's Practise: Exercises to apply the grammar rules taught, emphasizing on conceptual understanding

Grammar animations to further emphasize the concepts

Grammar games and interactivities to practise the concepts

4

Activity

Draw or paste photographs on the family tree below. Then, write who it is under each picture. Also write he or she correctly for each picture.

This is my family.

Activity: Fun, play-based activities that integrate art and lead to experiential learning

5

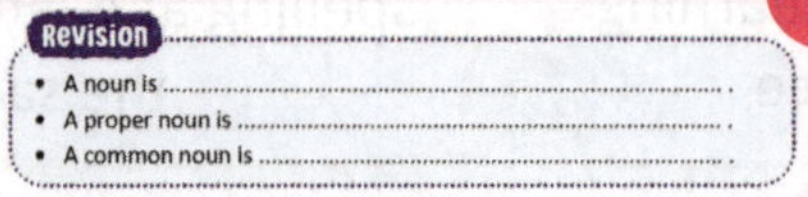

Revision

- A noun is ....
- A proper noun is ....
- A common noun is ....

Revision: Exercises to measure the learning outcomes

That's not all! Here are some more exciting features in the book!

Revision Tests in primary grades to check the previous knowledge

Competency-based **Test Papers** for regular assessments

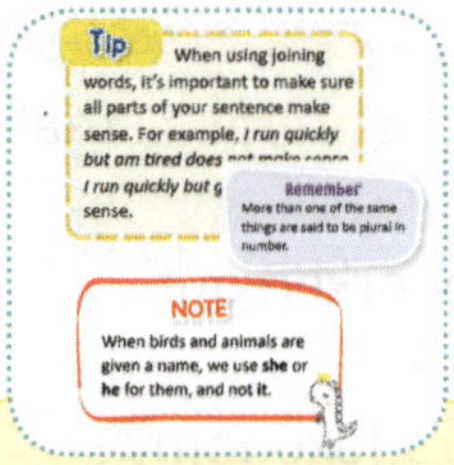

Tip: When using joining words, it's important to make sure all parts of your sentence make sense. For example, *I run quickly but am tired does not make sense.* *I run quickly but* ... sense.

Remember: More than one of the same things are said to be plural in number.

NOTE: When birds and animals are given a name, we use she or he for them, and not it.

Tips, Notes and **Remember** boxes to reiterate the rules and learn exceptions to the rules

Common Errors

A and An

We use a and an when we talk about one thing. We do not use a and an when we talk about more than one thing.

Common Errors to correct common grammar mistakes

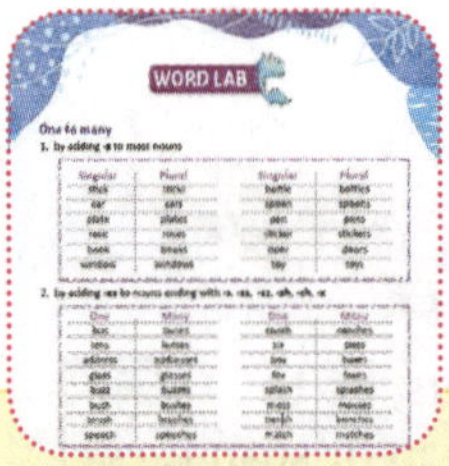

WORD LAB

One to many

Word Lab pages with extensive word lists

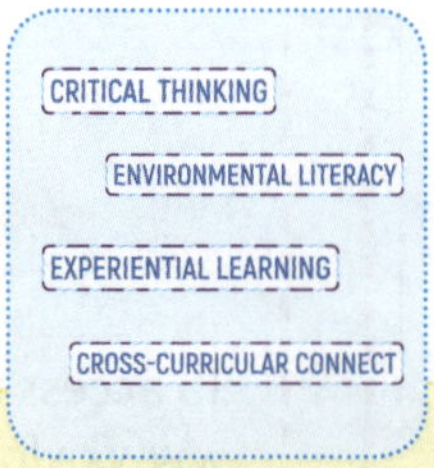

CRITICAL THINKING

ENVIRONMENTAL LITERACY

EXPERIENTIAL LEARNING

CROSS-CURRICULAR CONNECT

21st Century Skills and **NCF features** tagged in the books

Special Sections

Comprehension: Reading texts with questions in varied formats

Composition: Guided writing tasks with samples and formats

12. Adverbs	• Definition • Types of Adverbs	• Modifying verbs by using adverbs
13. Prepositions	• Definition • Types of Prepositions • Position of Prepositions • Objects of Prepositions • Group Prepositions • Collocation • Correct use of some Prepositions	• Expressing position, direction and time
14. Conjunctions	• Definition • List of Conjunctions: Functions	• Joining different grammatical units to form bigger units
15. Interjections	• Definition and usage	
Check Your Progress 3		
16. The Sentence	• Definition • Sentence and its parts: Subject and Predicate; Direct and Indirect Object	• Stating a fact, a feeling
17. Types of Sentences	• Identifying the different types	• Distinguishing between Affirmation, Negation, Asking questions, Command, Request, Advice and Expressing strong emotion
18. Phrases and Clauses	• Definition and types of phrases and clauses	• Understanding Phrases as units of language, and Clauses to make complete or partial proposition
19. Simple Sentence	• Definition • Difference between a sentence and a clause	• Expressing a complete meaning
20. Direct and Indirect Speech	• Direct Speech • Indirect Speech	• Reporting an event, recording an observation, making an evaluation
21. Punctuation	• Definition • Kinds of punctuation marks	• Understanding the functions of punctuation marks
22. Vocabulary	• Synonyms • Antonyms • Homophones	• Recognizing the building blocks of language in use
Check Your Progress 4		
Test Paper 2		
23. Comprehension	• Sample passages for practice from a variety of selections	
24. Composition	• Notices and Messages • Letters: personal letters, official letters • Diary Writing • Story Writing • Essay Writing	• Writing notices and phone messages • Writing personal and official letters • Writing diary entries • Writing stories from an outline or topic • Writing argumentative essays
Common Errors		
Word Lab		

Acknowledgements

Photographs

Bee, p. 9: © Theerapan/Shutterstock; Thrip, p. 9: © happymay/Shutterstock; Lacewing, p. 9 © SIMON SHIM/Shutterstock; Saina Nehwal, p. 32: © MARWAN NAAMANI/AFP/ Getty Images; Buckingham Palace, p. 37: © Neil Mitchell/Shutterstock; Taj Mahal, p. 52: © Grant Faint/Getty Images; Leaning Tower of Pisa, p. 52: © Adina Tovy/Getty Images; Chichen Itza, p. 52: © Fer Gregory/ Shutterstock; Pyramids of Egypt, p. 52: © Free Agents Limited/Getty Images; Christ the Redeemer, p. 52: © Christian Adams/Getty Images; Colosseum, p. 52: © Artie Photography (Artie Ng) /Getty Images; The Great Wall of China, p. 52: © DEA/W. BUSS/ Contributor/Getty Images; Dipa Karmakar, p. 55: © Patrick Smith/Getty Images; The Solar System, p. 58: © BSIP/ UIG/Getty Images; Red Fort, p. 89: © Welcome To The World Of My Photos. Enjoy !!!/Getty Images; Kolkata Town Hall, p. 110: © tantrik71/Shutterstock; Taj Mahal, p. 123: © Emad Aljumah/Getty Images; Mary Kom, p. 162: © Qamar Sibtain/The India Today Group/Getty Images; Golconda Fort, p. 185: © Thierry Falise/LightRocket via Getty Images; Mahatma and Kasturba Gandhi p. 200: © Mondadori Portfolio/Getty Image; Spotted Deer p. 202: © Panoramic Images/Getty Images; Sarus Crane p. 202: © David Tipling/Getty Images; Indian Museum in Kolkata p. 231: © Zvonimir Atletic/Shutterstock

1 The Noun

Let's Do

Given below is a passage about some insects that are not harmful. Read it.

Hi! I am Sanghita Basak. I would like to talk to you about helpful insects in your garden. Most people are either indifferent to, or scared of, insects and pests. But do you know all insects are not harmful and therefore should not be called pests? In fact, some of the pests that I'm going to talk about here are very helpful; they offer you a lot of help with gardening. If you love your garden, you should wait for these insects to invade it. My friend Diya does a lot of gardening in Pitampur in Bihar. She and her sister Riya have a big garden. They supply flowers, vegetables and fruits to Arani Supermarket. The last time we met, she told me certain things about helpful insects which I'm going to share with you.

The beautiful spotted ladybugs eat plant lice, a seriously harmful pest for the plants in your garden. The lacewings feed on caterpillars, moth eggs, mites and thrips. Though hoverflies look exactly like wasps and bees, they are very different from them. They too feed on insects and insect eggs and help us obtain bigger and juicier raspberries and strawberries.

Because Diya and Riya have made gardening their profession, they have to be careful. They don't like to use a lot of chemical pest repellent because that is harmful for harvest. They therefore depend on the harmless friendly insects. The long-legged, biggish ground beetles and garden spiders really like to feed on insects that seriously harm vegetables.

How many proper nouns and common nouns are there in the passage on page 9? Go back to the page and underline the proper nouns and circle the common nouns.

Let's Learn

A **noun** is a naming word. It is a word we use to name persons, other living beings, objects, places, ideas and feelings.

Nouns can be countable or uncountable.

- **Countable nouns** are the nouns that can be counted. These nouns can be used to answer the question *how many*?

  Examples: 1. How many *books* have you read?
  I have read *eight books*.
  2. How many *boys* are there in the group?
  There are *three boys* in the group.

In the examples, *books* and *boys* are countable nouns.

- **Uncountable nouns** are the nouns that cannot be counted. These nouns can be used to answer the question *how much*?

  Examples: 1. How much *sugar* do you want?
  I want *one teaspoonful sugar*.
  2. How much *water* is there in the bucket?
  There is a *lot of water* in the bucket.

In the examples, *sugar* and *water* are uncountable nouns.

There are different types of nouns—**proper, common, material, collective, concrete** and **abstract.**

Types of nouns

Nouns

- **Proper noun**: Rabindranath Tagore, New Delhi, Kaveri
- **Common noun**: woman, girl, doctor, city, teacher, shop, tennis
  - **Concrete noun**: flowers, songs, houses, tables, cookies
  - **Abstract noun**: beauty, charity, kindness, love, pity, courage
  - **Material noun**: silver, iron, sugar, flour, oil, wax, cotton
  - **Collective noun**: police, millitary, gang, family, crew, team

Now let us learn what each type of noun means.

- **Proper noun:** It is the name of a particular person, place or object. A proper noun always begins with a capital letter. For example, Kailash Satyarthi, Mumbai, Friday, etc.
- **Common noun:** It is the general name of persons, animals, things or objects. Common, from the Latin *communis*, means general, that is, belonging to all. For example, *ant, table,* etc.
- **Material noun:** It is the name of substances or materials. For example, *water, iron, steel, sugar, wood,* etc.

Remember

Though most **common nouns** are countable (they can be counted), **material nouns** are uncountable.

- **Collective noun:** It is the name given to a group or a class. For example, *mob, crew, jury, committee,* etc.
- **Concrete noun:** It is the name of things that can be experienced through the five senses that we have—sight, smell, hearing, taste and touch. For example, *sunrise, fragrance, fruit, rain, water*, etc.
- **Abstract noun:** It is the name of qualities, ideas, emotions, actions, feelings and conditions. These nouns are the names of things that cannot be seen, touched, heard, smelled or tasted. For example, *time, pride, love, ability,* etc.

Let's Practise

1. **Read the following passage and identify the nouns as proper, material and collective nouns and complete the table appropriately.**

The students of class VI of St Teresa's High School of Chennai started a project three months ago. Their class teacher asked each of them to take care of two plants at home. They planted tiny saplings in small steel pots which they filled with dry mud. Since plants need water to make their food using the sunlight, each of the little gardeners also bought small tin cans to water their plants. They put the plants outside during day so that the plants got enough sunlight. After coming back from school, they took the plants back into the shade to save the saplings from rain and excessive sunlight. Riaz from Section A and Rani from Section B led the project. Both kept a diary about the progress. Most students preferred flowers to vegetables or fruits. Many students planted marigolds, poppies and lilies, though only one student planted roses. Bunches of buds began to appear in some plants. There was only a group of four students in the entire class who decided to grow vegetables and fruits. Two students planted strawberries and are now expecting small bushel from the two plants. Other two students planted eggplants and now a pair of tiny eggplants has appeared. Everyone was very excited about this gardening project, especially now that their plants are flowering.

Proper	Material	Collective

2. a. **Listen to the Jataka tale about an elephant and a dog on the theme of friendship. After listening to the story, write down all the abstract nouns and concrete nouns in the table given below. Note that there are eight abstract nouns and seventeen concrete nouns in the story. Replay the audio and listen to it again if you miss out on any noun.**

Abstract nouns	Concrete nouns

b. **Now write down ten more abstract nouns here.**

....

....

Let's Learn

Formation of abstract nouns

Abstract nouns can also be made from other words, such as adjectives, common nouns and verbs. You can make new abstract nouns by adding suffixes to adjectives, common nouns and verbs.

Making abstract nouns from adjectives

It is possible to make new abstract nouns by adding the suffixes **-ness**, **-dom**, **-y**, etc. to an adjective.

Given below are some abstract nouns that are made from adjectives:

kind (adjective) + *-ness* (suffix) = kindness (abstract noun)

Some adjectives change differently to form abstract nouns:

long – length

humble – humility

Abstract nouns can be formed from verbs and other nouns as well:

friend (noun) – *friendship*

act (verb) – *action*

NOTE

If a word ends with *-y*, the *-y* will become *-i* after you add the suffix.

happy (adjective) + *-ness* (suffix) = happiness (abstract noun)

lazy (adjective) + *-ness* (suffix) = laziness (abstract noun)

Let's Practise

Provide abstract nouns for the following adjectives.

1. wise ....
2. courageous ....
3. brave ....
4. strong ....
5. sad ....
6. proud ....
7. intelligent ....
8. difficult ....
9. wide ....
10. silent ....

Let's Learn

Making abstract nouns from common nouns

It is possible to make new abstract nouns by adding the suffixes **-ship**, **-hood**, **-dom**, etc. to a common noun. Given below are some abstract nouns that are made from common nouns:

friend (common noun) + *-ship* (suffix) = friendship (abstract noun)
child (common noun) + *-hood* (suffix) = childhood (abstract noun)

Let's Practise

Add -ship, -hood or -dom to the given common nouns to make abstract nouns.

A	B
leader	
knight	
king	
scholar	
parent	
member	
sister	
partner	

Let's Learn

Making abstract nouns from verbs

New abstract nouns can also be made from verbs by adding suffixes such as **-ion**, **-ance**, **-iour**, **-ment**, **-ation**, **-al**, etc.

Examples: act (verb) + *-ion* (suffix) = action (abstract noun)
accept (verb) + *-ance* (suffix) = acceptance (abstract noun)
behave (verb) + *-iour* (suffix) = behaviour (abstract noun)
judge (verb) + *-ment* (suffix) = judgment (abstract noun)
invite (verb) + *-ation* (suffix) = invitation (abstract noun)
remove (verb) + *-al* (suffix) = removal (abstract noun)

NOTE

Some verbs have a different form of abstract nouns. You don't need to add any suffix to change them into an abstract noun. Some such words are:
die—death, lose—loss, sell—sale, speak—speech, etc.

Let's Practise

1. Some action words are given below. Change them into abstract nouns.

a.	see	....	g.	prevent	....
b.	attract	....	h.	injure	....
c.	discuss	....	i.	console	....
d.	argue	....	j.	assist	....
e.	agree	....	k.	attach	....
f.	locate	....	l.	approve	....

2. Change the following words into abstract nouns.

a. wise b. proud c. courageous d. intelligent e. famous f. neighbour g. know h. king i. glorious

a.	....	d.	....	g.	....
b.	....	e.	....	h.	....
c.	....	f.	....	i.	....

3. **Read the following passage. Fill in the blanks with appropriate abstract nouns from the list given below.**

compassion	bravery	panic	gratitude	strength
kindness	chaos	dedication	comfort	patience
leadership	danger	hope	courage	unity

Once upon a time, in a faraway village, there was a little girl named Saira who was known for her .... and .... Every day, she helped the elderly with their chores, showing great .... and .... One day, a fierce storm hit the village, causing much .... and .... among the villagers. Despite the ...., Saira's .... was intact. She organized a rescue team to help those in need. As the storm became fierce, the villagers found .... and .... in her .... Her actions brought .... and .... to the community. After the storm passed, the villagers celebrated with a feast, expressing their .... to Saira. Her .... had not only saved lives but also inspired others.

EXPERIENTIAL LEARNING

COLLABORATION AND COMMUNICATION

Activity

Do you like Spiderman? Following is a passage about him. Pick a partner and draw a web. Write *Spiderman* in the middle and in each concentric circle write the different types of nouns. Underline the nouns in the passage and then place them correctly in their correct circles in your web.

Spiderman is the name of the hero of a comic book series published from the United States of America in 1962. Stan Lee and Steve Ditko are the writer-editor and writer-artist who created this character. The actual name of the Spiderman is Peter Parker. He's an orphan. He is brought up by Aunt May and Uncle Ben. Both his uncle and aunt love him a lot. The Spiderman has the most amazing super powers. He can cling to any surface and spin webs from a device of his own invention. In real life, he is a boy who faces rejection and loneliness because he is shy and different.

2 Noun: Number

Let's Do

Nouns can be either **singular** or **plural** in number.

- A noun is **singular** in number when it indicates only one person, object or thing.
  Examples: *a man, a book, a pen, an apple, a chair, etc.*
- A noun is **plural** in number when it points to more than one person or thing.
  Examples: *five men, twenty pens, ten apples, fifteen chairs, etc.*

Remember

- Only countable nouns have plural forms. Singular countable nouns can be made plural usually by adding the suffix *-s* or *-es*. Nouns that are made plural by adding *-s* or *-es* are called regular nouns. For example, *table—tables, glass—glasses.*
- However, the plural forms of some nouns are made differently. Such nouns are called irregular nouns.

Forming plural nouns

Look at the following tables closely to learn about how we make plural forms of different nouns.

1. Plural forms of nouns ending in **-s, -ss, -ch, -sh,** and **-x.**

Singular	Plural	Singular	Plural
box	boxes	axe	axes
brush	brushes	kiss	kisses
bus	buses	match	matches
church	churches	lamp	lamps

All the above plural forms are made by adding **-s** or **-es** to the singular form of each noun. The structure of such plural form is as follows:

singular form + **-s/-es** = plural form

2. Plural forms of nouns ending in **-f** and **-fe**.

Singular	Plural
calf	calves
knife	knives
loaf	loaves
thief	thieves
self	selves
leaf	leaves

Remember

Nouns ending in either *-f* or *-fe* are made plural by adding *-ves* in place of *-f* or *-fe*. We can also see that the */f/* sound in these words changes into the */v/* sound.

However, there are some words which end in **-f** but do not follow the rule mentioned above. These words are made plural simply by adding **-s**.

The following is a list of such words:

Singular	Plural
chief	chiefs
proof	proofs
belief	beliefs
chef	chefs

Let's Practise

Change the number of the nouns given below.

1. donkey ....
2. calves ....
3. glass ....
4. sheaves ....
5. roof ....
6. holes ....
7. fly ....
8. machines ....
9. lily ....
10. pie ....
11. copy ....
12. stacks ....

Let's Learn

3. Plural forms of nouns ending in **-o**.

Singular	Plural	Singular	Plural
buffalo	buffaloes	echo	echoes
hero	heroes	mango	mangoes
mosquito	mosquitoes	potato	potatoes

Remember

Nouns ending in *-o* usually take *-es* at the end of the singular form to form their plural forms.

However, some words ending in **-o** do not follow the rule mentioned above. They take **-s** at the end and not **-es**.

Singular	Plural
eskimo	eskimos
photo	photos
piano	pianos
radio	radios
zero	zeros
studio	studios
ratio	ratios
stereo	stereos

4. If the last letter of a noun is **-y** and there is a consonant before the last letter, the last letter **-y** is changed into **-ies** in the plural form.

Examples: baby (singular)—bab*ies* (plural)
boy (singular)— boy*s* (plural)
story (singular)—stor*ies* (plural)
toy (singular)— toy*s* (plural)

Remember

- In the word *baby*, the consonant /*b*/ is placed before the last letter y. Therefore, the last letter *-y* in the singular form is replaced by *-ies* in its plural form.
- In the word *boy*, the vowel /*o*/ is placed before the last letter *-y*. Therefore, the letter y in this word is not changed. Only the usual plural marker *-s* is attached to make its plural form.

Look at the following table for more such words.

Singular	Plural
berry	berries
city	cities
dairy	dairies
army	armies
deity	deities
fairy	fairies

Let's Practise

Complete the following sentences by filling in the blanks with the correct form of the nouns given in brackets.

1. I watched three .... (film) last weekend.
2. The National Library has a .... (collection) of very rare .... (book).
3. After finishing their university education, the three .... (friend) started a company.
4. Add two .... (zero) after the number 5 to make it five hundred.
5. Jina wants to buy some .... (pen).
6. Ajit ate three stuffed .... (potato) for lunch.
7. The new Chinese restaurant in our locality brought five new .... (chef) from China.
8. Mother bought a bunch of .... (strawberry) last evening.

9. The .... (activity) conducted in the workshop were very helpful.
10. Dr Chawla's .... (theory) on nuclear power were published in The New Age Journal.
11. Amar baked five .... (loaf) of bread for our dinner party.
12. I had a dream about three .... (fairy) last night.

Let's Learn

Irregular plural forms

Some nouns do not follow the usual rules for forming their plurals. Sometimes these words change their spelling in a different way or do not change at all to make plurals.

1. Some nouns add **-en** or **-ren** to form their plural.

   Example: child (singular)—*children* (plural)

2. Some other nouns change their middle vowels to form their plurals.

   Example: foot (singular)—*feet* (plural)

   Look at the table below for more such irregular plural forms.

Singular	Plural
goose	geese
louse	lice
mouse	mice
tooth	teeth
man	men
woman	women
ox	oxen
policeman	policemen

3. The plural ending **-s** is added to the principal word in compound nouns.

   Example: sister-in-law (singular)—*sisters-in-law* (plural)

   Look at the table for more such words.

Singular	Plural	Singular	Plural
aunt-in-law	aunts-in-law	mother-in-law	mothers-in-law
commander-in-chief	commanders-in-chief	officer-in-charge	officers-in-charge
brother-in-law	brothers-in-law	runner-up	runners-up
father-in-law	fathers-in-law	son-in-law	sons-in-law

4. Some nouns have the same singular and plural forms. Look at the table below for some examples.

Singular	Plural
aircraft	aircraft
deer	deer
dozen	dozen
fish	fish
furniture	furniture
series	series
million	million
species	species
thousand	thousand

Remember

- Hundred, thousand and million have the same plural form as the singular only when they follow numerals.
  Examples: *five hundred pages,*
  ten thousand people,
  eight million rupees
- However, hundred, thousand and million have plural forms when they are referred in very large numbers.
  Examples: *hundreds of boxes,*
  thousands of books,
  millions of stars
- The names of nationality ending in *-ese* do not change in the plural forms. Therefore, nouns such as Chinese or Japanese remain the same in their plural form.

5. Foreign plurals—Some words in English have been borrowed from other languages. These words are called **loan words**. Formation of plurals for such words is different from the usual rules.

   Look at the words below which have been borrowed either from Greek or Latin.

Singular	Plural
agendum	agenda
analysis	analyses
appendix	appendices
curriculum	curricula
formula	formulae
basis	bases
crisis	crises
criterion	criteria
oasis	oases
phenomenon	phenomena

Let's Practise

Change the nouns given in brackets to their plural forms. Remember to capitalize, when necessary.

1. Make five .... (sheaf) of sticks from this pile.
2. .... (mosquito) can cause malaria.
3. .... (officer-in-charge) are going to visit our unit this week.
4. Brush at least twice a day to keep your .... (tooth) in good shape.
5. The .... (analysis) of the science and mathematics .... (curriculum) have been done by our teachers.
6. There are very few .... (leaf) left on the tree.
7. Where are the .... (proof) in support of your claim?
8. .... (lady and gentleman), I welcome you to this gathering.
9. Two of my sister's .... (brother-in-law) are visiting us today.
10. The value of human .... (life) is enormous.

Let's Learn

6. The names of objects that have two essential parts are always used in the plural. Such words cannot be used in their singular form. Therefore, we need to use plural verbs with them. **Examples:** *binoculars, glasses, jeans, pyjamas, pants, pliers, scales, scissors, tongs, trousers*, etc.
7. Some nouns ending in either **-s** or **-ics** are usually singular uncountable nouns and have no plural forms. **Example:** *Linguistics* is my favourite subject.
   Here, the word *linguistics*, though it appears to be in its plural form is actually a singular uncountable noun. Therefore, it has no plural form. The verbs that go with these words are always singular. **Examples:** *aerobics, Biophysics, gymnastics, Mathematics, stylistics, measles, news, Physics, politics, Statistics*, etc.

Remember

We need to use appropriate verbs according to the number of the noun we use.

8. Uncountable nouns, such as *advice, furniture, information*, do not have a plural form.
9. Abstract nouns, such as *admiration, affection, hatred, love*, and material nouns, such as *iron, sugar, silk, wood* are not countable nouns. Therefore, they do not have any plural form.

10. An apostrophe followed by **-s** is added to figures such as *1*, *2*, *3* and letters, such as *a*, *b*, *c* in their plural forms.

Examples: a. Please write your *t's* clearly.

b. Underline all the number *5's* in 257785205.

11. Some collective nouns such as *people* and *cattle* look like singular nouns though they denote a plural concept. Therefore, they take plural verbs.

Let's Practise

Fill in the blanks in the following sentences with appropriate forms of words given in brackets.

1. The people in the queue .... very impatient. (be)
2. Her affection for you .... to be absolutely selfless. (appear)
3. Gita's favourite subject .... Physics. (be)
4. Your jeans .... really good. (look)
5. These glasses .... been lying here for ages. (have)
6. This advice .... not going to be very helpful. (be)
7. .... your new furniture arrived? (have)
8. Steel .... made of iron. (be)
9. Leaves of deciduous plants ....
(change) colour during autumn.
10. Mina's love for her pet dog .... (be) admirable.

COLLABORATION AND COMMUNICATION | CREATIVE THINKING | CRITICAL THINKING

Activity

Make groups of four and write a short dialogue. You must include countable/uncountable nouns (both singular and plural forms). Keep a note of how many you have used. Act it out in front of the class. The other groups must watch out for the countable and uncountable nouns and keep a count. Whichever team manages to identify the most number of nouns wins.

3 Noun: Gender

Let's Learn

Gender is the feature of a noun or a pronoun that classifies it as masculine, feminine, common or neuter gender.

Example: My sister Soma and Mr Bukhari's son Susheel are friends. They went to the same school.

In the above sentences,

- the word *sister* tells us that the person being spoken of is a woman.
- the word *son* tells us that the person being spoken of is a man.
- *friends* tells us that the persons being spoken of can be either male or female.
- *school* tells us that the noun is an inanimate thing and is neither male nor female.

Thus, by merely looking at the words we know whether

- someone is a male or female.
- it is a non-living thing or living thing.
- it is a class name that can refer to both male and female.

The feature that helps us to identify the above in nouns is called **gender**. The English language has four genders.

Gender

- **Masculine:** Refers to males. **Example:** man
- **Feminine:** Refers to females. **Example:** woman
- **Common:** Refers to either males or females. **Example:** student
- **Neuter:** Refers to a non-living thing that is neither male nor female. **Example:** car

Let's Practise

Identify the masculine and feminine nouns in the following passage. Circle the masculine and underline the feminine nouns.

Tom was to arrive early in the afternoon. Mrs Tulliver and Maggie were waiting anxiously for the sounds of the carriage wheels. At last the sound came—that quick, light bowling of the wheels—and, in spite of the wind, Mrs Tulliver came outside the door to greet her boy. Mrs Tulliver stood with her arms open. Maggie jumped first on one leg and then on the other; while Tom descended from the carriage and said, "Hallo! Yap—what! are you there?" Nevertheless, he allowed his mother and sister to kiss him. While Maggie hung on his neck in rather a strangling fashion, his blue-grey eyes wandered towards the river where he promised himself that he would begin to fish the first thing the next morning. He was one of those lads that grow everywhere in England and, at twelve or thirteen years of age, look as much alike as goslings—a lad with light brown hair, cheeks of cream and roses, full lips, indeterminate nose and eyebrows.

Let's Learn

Feminine gender can be formed in different ways.

1. By adding **-ess** to the masculine form.

Examples:

Masculine	Feminine
actor	actress
duke	duchess
emperor	empress
governor	governess
host	hostess
hunter	huntress
waiter	waitress
lion	lioness
tiger	tigress

Remember

In the examples, the addition of *-ess* causes an internal change in the spelling of the word.

2. By using a completely different word.

Masculine	Feminine	Masculine	Feminine
brother	sister	bull	cow
cock	hen	colt	filly
dad	mom	lad	lass
father	mother	fox	vixen
gander	goose	groom	bride
horse	mare	husband	wife
lord	lady	man	woman
monk	nun	nephew	niece
son	daughter	uncle	aunt

3. By the formation of compound words, that is, by adding another word to the feminine noun.

Examples: *washer + man = washerman (masculine)*

washer + woman = washerwoman (feminine)

Masculine	Feminine	Masculine	Feminine
fisherman	fisherwoman	grandfather	grandmother
grandson	granddaughter	granduncle	grandaunt
he-goat	she-goat	landlord	landlady
manservant	maidservant	milkman	milkmaid
stepfather	stepmother	stepson	stepdaughter

4. Some words have a slightly different form than those mentioned earlier for their feminine genders.

Masculine	Feminine
hero	heroine
master	mistress
lad	lass
widower	widow

Let's Practise

1. Change the gender of the underlined words from masculine to feminine and feminine to masculine.

a. My father is the only man in the neighbourhood who can fly a helicopter.

....

b. The mistress of the house acted as the hostess.

....

c. Gita owns a mare, a goose and a rooster.

....

d. The Duke's sisters looked after him.

....

e. Tigers look after their cubs.

....

f. The hero went to England to meet the king.

....

g. The milkmaid lost her he-goat yesterday.

....

h. The master of the feast asked the steward to serve the food.

....

2. Look at the pictures to help you fill in the blanks.

a. The female sheep is called ....

i. ewe   ii. sheep   iii. lamb

b. My uncle is getting married. The name of his .... is Sunita.

i. mother   ii. bride   iii. sister

c. Mr Rasheed has two .... called Ali and Sameer.

i. sons   ii. daughters   iii. aunts

d. The queen's daughter is called a ....

i. prince   ii. king   iii. princess

e. Uncle Bose is my father's ....

i. sister   ii. brother   iii. uncle

f. Uncle Bose's wife is an ....

i. actress   ii. actor   iii. headmaster

g. Zubeida helped the old .... cross the road.

i. boy   ii. man   iii. lady

h. These two children are ....

i. girls   ii. friends   iii. sisters

i. A .... has a shorter tail than a peacock.

i. hen   ii. peahen   iii. gander

j. Mr Mondal is a .... of many talents.

i. man   ii. boy   iii. lady

Let's Learn

Common and neuter gender

Common gender refers to either male or female.

Look at the list of words denoting common gender.

footballer	friend	anchor	announcer
individual	organizer	baby	child
parent	person	companion	composer
player	pupil	cousin	cricketer

Neuter gender refers to non-living things that are neither male nor female.

quilt	book	chair
taxi	desk	egg
van	gold	hat
school	ink	kite
umbrella	lamp	mat
watch	net	pot

Remember

Though collective nouns such as *army*, *team*, *flock*, *class*, and *group* are used to signify the collection or group of living things, they are classified as *neuter gender*.

Let's Practise

1. Read the following extract from a story. Identify words denoting masculine (M), feminine (F), common (C) and neuter (N) genders.

"Well, dearies, how have you got on today? Has anyone called, Beth? How is your cold, Meg? Jo, you look tired to death. Come and kiss me, children."

While making these maternal inquiries Mrs March got her wet things off, her warm slippers on, and sitting down in the easy chair, preparing to enjoy the happiest hour of her busy day. The girls flew about, trying to make things comfortable, each in her own way. Meg arranged the tea table, Jo brought wood clattering everything she touched. Beth trotted to and fro between parlour and kitchen, while Amy gave directions to everyone, as she sat with her hands folded.

As they gathered about the table, Mrs March said, with a particularly happy face, "I've got a treat for you after supper."

A quick, bright smile went round like a streak of sunshine. Beth clapped her hands, and Jo tossed up her napkin, crying, "A letter! A letter! Three cheers for Father!"

"Yes, a nice long letter. He is well and sends all sorts of loving wishes for Christmas, and a special message to you girls," said Mrs March.

2. Identify the gender of the underlined nouns as masculine, feminine, common and neuter. Write them in the right columns in the table that follows.

a. Mita is my cousin and Sajal is my brother.
b. Red Riding Hood met a wolf in the forest.
c. Gita walks to school with her friends.
d. My son loves his dog.
e. Mrs Avasty is such a skilled dancer and actress.
f. George is a good public speaker. But he has a bad stage fright.
g. I forgot my pencil at home.
h. My uncle and aunt work in a factory with other workers.

Masculine	Feminine	Common	Neuter

Check Your Progress 1

1. Identify the nouns in the following passage and write them down in the table below. Write five words under each heading–proper nouns, common nouns, collective nouns, abstract nouns.

KNOWLEDGE OF INDIA

Saina Nehwal is the first Indian woman to be ranked as number one in Badminton World Federation in Women's Singles category. She was born in Hisar on March 17, 1990. She attended Campus School CCS HAU, Hisar and later shifted to Hyderabad with her family. She has represented India three times in the Olympics, winning a bronze medal in her second appearance. She achieved the Bronze medal at the London Olympics 2014. Nehwal was the first Indian to win the World Junior Badminton Championship and the first Indian to win a Super Series tournament and the Indonesian Open in 2009. She led a team to the 2010 Uber Cup. This outstanding Indian sportsperson had reached the finals of the All England Open Badminton on 7 March, 2015. Her achievements caused an increasing popularity of badminton in India. Her journey is an inspiration to groups of young boys and girls. The Government of India conferred a Padma Bhushan award on her in 2016. She has made the nation proud through her performances.

Proper noun	Common noun	Collective noun	Abstract noun

2. Write the plural forms of the following nouns. Use the plural forms in sentences of your own.

Singular	Plural	Singular	Plural
piano		mango	
candle		diary	
judge		shelf	
eskimo		proof	
country		toy	
mouse		son-in-law	

3. Given below are some nouns belonging to masculine, feminine, common, or neuter gender. Fill in the blanks in the passage with the correct form of noun as per the instruction provided in brackets.

dog	wife	scenery	sister	home	children
food	postman	table	husband	daughter	
farmer	artist	man	baby	family	

A (masculine) .... called John Singh lived in Rampur. He was known as the best (common) .... in the area. John Singh had a loyal (common) .... named Max, who followed him everywhere. Max loved to play with the village (common) .... whenever they visited the farm. John Singh had a (feminine) .... named Lily. She was a talented budding (common) .... who loved to paint the beautiful (neuter) .... around the farm. One day, a (masculine) .... delivered a letter to John Singh. The letter was from his (feminine) .... who lived in the city. She was coming to visit with her (masculine) .... and their (common) .... When the family arrived, John Singh and his (feminine) .... prepared a delicious meal for their guests. They all sat around the (neuter) ...., enjoyed the (neuter) ...., and chatted for hours. The whole (common) .... had a wonderful time together, enjoying the warmth and love that filled their (neuter) ....

4 Articles

Let's Learn

Words *a*, *an* and *the* are known as **articles**. An article always comes before the noun in a sentence.

Articles are of two types—indefinite and definite articles.

Articles
- **Indefinite** (a, an)
- **Definite** (the)

Indefinite articles

An **indefinite article** appears before a common noun.

Read the following passage.

> I have *a* friend in New Delhi. He sings very well and I thought he would want to become *a* singer in future. But he wants to become *an* artist when he grows up. Last week he sent me *a* painting done by him.

In the above passage, the articles **a** and **an** come before nouns such as *friend, singer, painting*, and *artist*. These nouns stand for a whole class of persons or objects. They are also called common nouns. Articles **a** and **an** are used to indicate just one member or object of the class of common nouns. The articles **a** or **an** mean one.

A and **an** refer to any one general member of a class of common nouns. Therefore, they are called **indefinite articles**.

When do we use indefinite articles?

We use **a** and **an**

- before countable nouns in their singular form.
  Examples: *a* student, *a* chair, *an* ant, *an* apple
- to refer to a member of a class or type of people, things, etc.
  Examples: *an* engineer, *a* mobile phone, etc.
- when a proper noun is used as a common noun.
  Example: We need *a* Gandhi to stop violence in India now.
- in some expressions that contain idioms.
  Example: Mukul was in *a* hurry.

Remember

A is used before a noun beginning with a consonant sound and *an* is used before a noun beginning with a vowel sound.

Examples: *a* friend, *an* artist

We **do not** use **a** and **an**

- before countable nouns in their plural forms and before uncountable nouns because **a** and **an** signify 'one'.
  Examples: I have chairs in my study. NOT ... ~~a chairs~~.
  Please bring some sugar. NOT ... ~~a sugar~~.
- before an adjective not followed by a noun.
  Example: "He is brilliant". NOT ... ~~He is a brilliant~~.
- when the noun is preceded by another determiner.
  Examples: This is a poem of mine. NOT ... ~~This is a my poem~~.
  Have you seen a movie recently? NOT ... ~~Have you seen a any movie recently?~~

NOTE

Determiners are words which modify a noun in some way. Some other determiners are: *this, that, these, those, my, your, his, either, neither, some, any, many, what, whose.*

Let's Practise

Fill in the blanks with appropriate indefinite articles. If no article is required, write X.

1. This is .... ostrich.
2. I just finished reading .... book.
3. The students need help with shifting .... almirah.
4. We need to take the patient to .... hospital.
5. Rima wants .... boiled egg for breakfast.
6. Please bring me .... umbrella.
7. Rahul is .... naughty.
8. Diya's elder sister is studying in .... university in the USA.

Let's Learn

Definite articles

A **definite article** is used when we want to refer to a particular person or object.

Read the following passage.

We usually complete *an* exercise or *a* task within ten minutes. But *the* exercise we are doing today will take *a* little more time. *The* time within which we must complete *the* exercise is fifteen minutes.

In the above passage, the words **an** and **a** refer to *exercises* and *tasks* in general.

The word **the** refers to a particular *exercise* or *task* that the teacher wants the students to do that day. It also refers to a specific period of time given to them to complete the task.

When do we use definite articles?

We use *the* with

- singular nouns
  Example: *The* exercise you did today was difficult.
- plural nouns
  Example: *The* exercises in this chapter are very interesting.
- nouns already mentioned
  Example: I'm writing *a* poem now. *The* poem is about nature.
- uncountable nouns when a particular or definite reference is made to them
  Example: *The* milk is stale.
- ordinals such as first, second, third, next, further, etc.
  Example: *The* first letter of the English alphabet is 'A'.
- adjectives in the superlative degree
  Example: Asif is *the* best athlete in our school team.
  Mount Everest is *the* highest peak in the world.
- musical instruments
  Example: *the drums, the guitar*
- names of
  - seas, oceans and rivers
    Example: *the* Ganges, *the* Bay of Bengal

- some countries

  Example: *the* United Arab Emirates, *the* United States of America

- mountain ranges

  Examples: *the* Alps, *the* Himalayas
- well-known buildings

  Examples: *the* Red Fort, *the* Buckingham Palace
- newspapers

  Examples: *the* Hindu, *the* Deccan Herald
- trains, ships

  Examples: *the* Darjeeling Mail, *the* MV Harshavardhana

Remember

We do not use any article with

- proper nouns, such as *India*, *Mr Rajbir Singh*, etc.
- abstract nouns, such as *honesty*, *beauty*, *truthfulness*, etc.
- material nouns, such as *iron*, *steel*, *sugar*, etc.
- common nouns in idiomatic expressions such as *go by bus*, *travel by taxi*, *be out of station*, *feel at home*, etc.

Let's Practise

1. In the following statements definite articles have been omitted. Insert them wherever necessary.

a. I learnt to play trumpet when I was 6 years old.

b. Bay of Bengal, Indian ocean and Arabian Sea are three water bodies that surround India at south eastern, south western and southern territories.

c. Taj Mahal is one of seven wonders of world.

d. Rabindranath Tagore is national poet of India. He received Nobel Prize for literature in 1913. He returned knighthood as a protest against Jalianwala Bagh Massacre in 1919.

....

....

2. Fill in the blanks in the following sentences using a/an/the/X.

a. To get to our school, cross .... street, walk three blocks towards .... east and you'll see .... school right in .... corner.

b. .... elephant has escaped from .... zoo. It has taken shelter in .... nearby school. Everyone in .... neighbourhood seems to be extremely scared. No one is ready to face .... elephant. .... zoo officials have been called to capture .... elephant.

c. .... trees are crucial to human existence on .... earth. Yet we are bent upon destroying .... forests. Indiscriminate cutting of trees in the Himalayan forest is .... root cause of soil erosion.

3. Read the following story from Aesop's fables. The articles are missing in the story. Complete the story with correct articles choosing from those given in brackets.

.... (A/An/The) eagle was flying high through .... (a/an/the) air when suddenly it heard .... (a/an/the) arrow whizzing in. Immediately after that it felt itself seriously wounded. It didn't know what exactly hurt it. Slowly it fluttered down to .... (a/an/the) earth, with its life-blood pouring out of .... fresh wound. Trying to tend .... (a/an/the) wound it saw .... (a/an/the) arrow sticking out. While looking closely at .... (a/an/the) arrow .... (a/an/the) eagle saw .... (a/an/the) feather in .... (a/an/the) shaft of .... (a/ an/the) arrow. .... (a/an/the) eagle knew it is .... (a/an/the) feather from its own body. It exclaimed with sorrow, "Alas! How we hand in to our enemies .... (a/an/the) instrument that can harm us."

5 Pronouns

Let's Learn

A **pronoun** is a word that is used in place of a noun. We can replace a noun with a pronoun.

Read the passages given below.

Passage A:

Anita has an 11-year-old son called *Ratan*. *Anita* and *Ratan* live in Kolkata. *Ratan* studies in Class VI. *Ratan* loves to browse the *Internet*. *Ratan* introduced *Ratan's mother* to the *Internet*. *Anita* now uses Anita and Ratan's computer whenever *Anita* finds time.

Passage A gives us some information about Anita and her son Ratan. This passage is monotonous because the names, *Anita*, *Ratan*, *the Internet*, *Ratan's mother*, are repeated several times.

Passage B:

Anita has an 11-year-old son called Ratan. *They* live in Kolkata. Ratan studies in Class VI. *He* loves to browse the Internet. *He* introduced *his mother* to *it*. *She* now uses *their* computer whenever *she* finds time.

In passage B, nouns are replaced by some other words given in italics. These words are called *pronouns*. *Pronouns* such as *he*, *she*, *they*, *his*, *their*, *it* replace nouns such as *Ratan*, *Anita*, *Ratan and Anita*, *Ratan's*, *Anita and Ratan's*, and *the Internet*. By using pronouns, the monotony of expression in the passage is reduced.

A pronoun occupies the same position as a noun in a sentence. Like a noun, a pronoun also plays the role of a subject, direct object and indirect object in a sentence. It shares similar grammatical characteristics with nouns.

For example, like a noun, a pronoun also should agree with the verb in the sentence in gender and number.

Let's Practise

In the following passage, a few pronouns have been left out. Insert a slash (/) where you think a pronoun is missing and write the pronouns in the blanks given.

Ananya, Manu and Sophiya are in New York. Today are going to the Museum ....
of Modern Art. Sophiya has been there before. had loved the place and told ....
the others. sister, Ananya, does not care too much about art. Manu has always ....
been interested in art. is most excited among the three friends. MoMA has ....
a great collection of artworks. The three of will see Van Gogh's 'Starry Night'. ....
is a magnificent piece of art. Vincent Van Gogh was a 19th century Dutch painter. ....
style of art is known as Post-Impressionist. The three friends will have a very ....
memorable experience today.

Let's Learn

Types of pronouns

Pronouns are of different types. The following diagram lists the different types of pronouns.

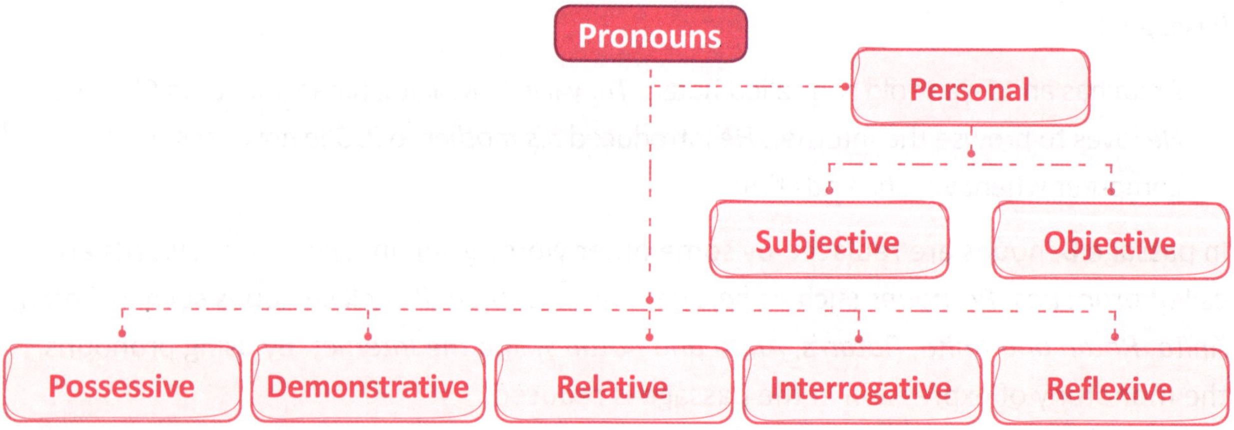

Personal pronouns

Read passage B once again.

> Anita has an 11-year-old son called Ratan. *They* live in Kolkata. Ratan studies in Class VI. *He* loves to browse the Internet. *He* introduced *his mother* to *it*. *She* now uses their computer whenever *she* finds time.

In passage B, the pronouns *he*, *she*, *they*, and *it* replace the nouns. *Ratan*, *Anita*, *Ratan* and *Anita*, *Anita* and *Ratan's* and *the Internet*.

Personal pronouns stand for three **persons**.

1. The first person—*I* and *we*
2. The second person—*you*
3. The third person—*he*, *she*, *it*, *they*

Remember

In the passage you read, the nouns that the pronouns (*he*, *she*, *they*, *it*) replace are: either persons (*Anita*, *Ratan*) or things (*the Internet*).

Personal pronouns are of two types.

1. **Subjective**—Pronouns that act as the subject of a sentence such as *I*, *you*, *he*, *she*, etc.
2. **Objective**—Pronouns that act as the object of a verb or a preposition in a sentence such as *me*, *him*, *her*, etc.

Look at the following sentences.

Simi's best friend is Sohail. *She* likes *him* very much. *He* is also very fond of *her*.

In the sentences given above,

- the pronouns *she* and *he* act as the subject. Therefore, they are **personal subjective pronouns.**
- *Him* in the second sentence and *her* in the third sentence act as the object of the verb *like* and of the preposition *of* respectively. Hence, they are **personal objective pronouns.**

The following table gives the different forms of personal pronouns.

Person	Number				Gender		
	singular		plural		masculine	feminine	neuter
	subjective	objective	subjective	objective			
first	I	me	we	us	✓	✓	
second	you	you	you	you	✓	✓	
third	he	him			✓		
	she	her				✓	
			they	them	✓	✓	✓
	it	it					✓

Let's Practise

Amira is a 12-year-old girl. She is introducing her family to us in the following sentences. Personal pronouns are missing in these sentences. Fill in the blanks and complete Amira's story about her family.

My name is Amira. .... am the youngest in the family. This is my father. .... is a doctor. This is my mother. .... runs a business. This is my brother Azim. .... is older than me. .... looks after our cat and dog. .... loves .... very much. .... go to the same school. Mr Roth is our class teacher. Everyone likes .... teaches .... Science. This is our garden. .... look after ....

Let's Learn

Possessive pronouns

In passage B, pronouns such as *his* and *hers*, denote **possession**. These two words tell you who something belongs to. In this passage, these two words refer to the computer that **belongs** to Ratan and Anita respectively.

- *his* and *hers*—refers to the computer **belonging to Anita and Ratan.**

> Pronouns that help us show possession or belonging are called possessive pronouns.
> Words such as *mine, ours, yours, his, hers, theirs* are **possessive pronouns.**

The following table gives the different forms of possessive pronouns.

Person	Number		Gender		
	singular	plural	masculine	feminine	neuter
first	mine	ours	✓	✓	
second	yours	yours	✓	✓	

third	his		✓		
	hers			✓	
		theirs	✓	✓	

It is easy to confuse possessive pronouns and adjectives. Look at the table given below to see the difference.

Person	Pronoun	Adjective
1st singular	mine	my
2nd	yours	your
3rd (female)	hers	her
3rd (male)	his	his
3rd (neutral)	its	its
1st plural	ours	our
3rd plural	theirs	their

Remember

- The personal pronoun *it* is used to refer to an animal, a thing, or a child.

  Examples: The child is crying. *It* must be hungry.

  He kicked the ball hard. *It* went flying to the goalpost.
- We use *it* also as a dummy subject.

  Example: *It* is a fine day.

Using possessive pronouns and adjectives:

A possessive pronoun is used instead of a noun:

Example: Julie's car is red. Mine is blue.

A possessive adjective is usually used to describe a noun, and it comes before it, like other adjectives:

Example: My car is bigger than her car.

Let's Practise

From the pronouns given in brackets, choose the right one to complete each sentence below.

1. You can take these cookies if you want. They are .... (my/mine/me).
2. While Madhu and I are still looking at our homework, Anil completed .... (his/her/him) long ago.
3. Madhu did not even start .... (his/her/hers) yet.

4. We must finish our work quickly. I'm doing .... (my/mine/ours) and you should do .... (yours/your/you).
5. I didn't have a racket to play badminton with. So, my friend Riju gave me .... (his/hers/theirs).
6. I saw this bag lying in the field. Is it .... (your/yours/you)?
7. The colour of my bag is blue. This is not .... (my/mine/me).
8. Rita was looking for her bag too. It may be .... (her/hers/his).

Let's Learn

Interrogative pronouns

Look at the words in italics in the following sentences.

1. *Who* is the President of India?
2. *Which* is mightier, the pen or the sword?
3. *Whose* is this dog?
4. *What* is your name?
5. *Whom* would you like to meet?

NOTE

- Like demonstrative pronouns, some interrogative pronouns can also act both as interrogative adjectives and as interrogative pronouns.
- When these words qualify nouns they act as interrogative adjectives.
- When they stand for the persons or things about whom or which the questions are asked, they act as interrogative pronouns.

Pronouns which are used to ask questions are called **interrogative pronouns**. There are five interrogative pronouns: *who*, *what*, *whose*, *which*, and *whom*.

Look at the following questions.

1. What is your name?
2. What city did you grow up in?
3. Which book do you plan to read?
4. Which is the book you like most?

In sentences 1 and 4, words such as *what* and *which* stand for the nouns *name* and *book*. Therefore, they are *interrogative pronouns*.

Remember

- *Who* is used only for persons.
  Example: *Who* will be the next President?
- *Which* is used for things.
  Example: *Which* is your room?
- *What* is used only for things.
  Example: *What* are you searching for?

But the same words in Sentences (2) and (3) qualify the nouns *name* and *book*. Therefore, they act as *interrogative adjectives*.

Let's Practise

1. Fill in the blanks with suitable interrogative pronouns.

a. .... is your cat's name?
b. .... are you waiting for?
c. .... is this umbrella?
d. .... is your staple diet?
e. .... is late for the class today?
f. .... showed you the way to school?
g. .... is your favourite book?
h. .... is your carton, the small one or the other?
i. .... have you invited?
j. .... is more important, food or film?

Tip

If there is a noun after *which* or *what*, it is an interrogative adjective.

When *which* or *what* is used on its own with a following noun, it is an interrogative pronoun.

2. Read the following sentences and underline the interrogative pronouns and interrogative adjectives. Write IP for interrogative pronouns and IA for interrogative adjectives. One has been done for you.

a. Which play is to be performed in the annual function? ....IA..........
b. What do you want to say? ....
c. Who is the composer of the Indian National Anthem? ....
d. Who is your best friend in this class? ....
e. Which student cannot sing our National Anthem correctly? ....
f. What is the colour of your bag—blue or red? ....
g. Whose responsibility is it to collect the litter from the field today? ....
h. Whose book is lying on the floor? ....
i. Which season is your favourite? ....
j. We can order either Chinese or Indian food. What do you prefer? ....

Let's Learn

Reflexive pronouns

Read the following sentences.

1. The cat fell from a tree and hurt *itself*.
2. I cursed *myself* for going late to the examination hall.

3. "I hope you enjoy yourselves at the school picnic," his mother said.
4. We often have to blame *ourselves* for our failure.

Words such as *itself*, *myself*, *yourself* and *ourselves* are the objects of the verb in the sentences. But they refer to the same person as the subject does. The 'self' forms of personal pronouns are called **reflexive pronouns**.

A **reflexive pronoun** cannot be used as the subject of a sentence. We cannot say—*Myself want to join the army*.

The following table gives the different forms of reflexive pronouns.

Person	Number				Gender		
	singular		plural		masculine	feminine	neuter
	personal	reflexive	personal	reflexive			
first	I	myself	we	ourselves	✓	✓	
second	you	yourself	you	yourselves	✓	✓	
third	he	himself			✓		
	she	himself				✓	
			they	themselves	✓	✓	
	it	itself					✓

Let's Practise

Fill in the blanks with appropriate reflexive pronouns. One has been done for you.

1. She cares only for ....herself.............. and not for others.
2. The boys are always quarrelling among ....
3. An automatic computer works by ....
4. "Ladies and gentlemen please help .... to the food," said the host to her guests.
5. Ali, please dry .... immediately, otherwise you'll catch a cold.
6. We .... are to be blamed for this trouble.
7. They found their way to the college ....
8. Tania made her dinner all by ....
9. The rat looked at .... in the mirror.
10. We made .... sick by eating too much at the picnic.

6 Demonstrative and Relative Pronouns

Let's Learn

Demonstrative pronouns

Read the following passage.

"*Those* are the books that my aunt gave me and *that* is the pen which my uncle bought for me in 2022. *This* is my stock of treasures," said Mitin to Somu, pointing to her study table. "I cannot think of giving *these* away to anybody," she said to him.

Words such as *this*, *that*, *these*, and *those* are used as **demonstrative pronouns**. They are called **demonstrative pronouns** when they stand for a noun.

In the above passage, **demonstrative pronouns** such as *these*, *that*, *this* and *those* are used to point to some particular person or thing.

- *Those* stands for *Mitin's books*.
- *That* refers to *Mitin's pen*.
- *This* stands for *Mitin's stock of treasures*.
- *These* points to *Mitin's treasures*.

Examples:

1. I am looking for a bookshelf, but *this* one won't fit in my study.
   This refers to the *bookshelf*.
2. I went to see the movie, but *that* was not possible.
   That refers *to see the movie*.

Remember

- *This*, *that*, *these* and *those* can act as both demonstrative pronouns and demonstrative adjectives.
  Examples: 1. *This* is my book. (demonstrative pronoun)
  2. *This* book is mine. (demonstrative adjective)
- Demonstrative pronouns replace a noun.
- Demonstrative adjectives qualify a noun and answer the question which.

Demonstrative pronouns such as *this* and *that* sometimes refer to what is said in a whole sentence or clause.

Distinguishing demonstrative pronouns from demonstrative adjectives

- The demonstrative adjective is **always** followed by a noun:

  Example:

  I wanted to watch this (Adj) movie (Noun).

- The demonstrative pronoun **replaces** a noun phrase:

  Example:

  I went to see the movie, but ~~watching the movie~~ THAT (pronoun) was not possible.

Let's Practise

Identify the demonstrative adjectives and demonstrative pronouns in the following story. Make separate lists of phrases containing demonstrative adjectives and demonstrative pronouns. One has been done for you.

This (demonstrative adjective) story was told by my grandmother when I was in Class VI. This is a story of a brave girl. The girl lived in a small village with her family. In that village, there was no electricity in those days. One evening, she was playing with her brother in the courtyard and he suddenly shouted "Sister, look at those shadows—those are ghosts!" The little girl looked up and saw her brother pointing towards their garden.

"Those are only trees," she said, with a smile. She was also scared but she didn't say that to her brother. After her brother went to bed at night she came out of her house silently. She walked towards the garden. This was a night of full moon and there was moonlight everywhere. Slowly she entered the garden and went near the place where her brother saw those shadows. As soon as she reached there, she burst into loud laughter. "So that was my brother's ghost!" she thought. Do you know what she saw? It was the shadow of a tall banana plant with frayed leaves. This plant was moving to and fro in the breeze. In the pale evening light, this plant's shadow had appeared to be a woman wearing a hood and dancing.

Let's Learn

Relative pronouns

Pronouns that are used to introduce relative clauses are called relative pronouns. Relative pronouns link phrases or clauses to another in a sentence.

Words such as *who*, *whom*, *that*, *which*, *when*, and *where* are **relative pronouns**.

These pronouns are used often to introduce dependent and/or relative clauses in sentences.

Look at the following sentence:

The boy *who stood first in the CBSE examination* **is my cousin.**

The main sentence, given in bold is *the boy is my cousin* and the relative clause given in italics is *who stood first in CBSE examination*.

The relative clause gives additional information about the *boy*. The sentence talks about a particular boy who stood first in the CBSE examinations. The relative clause gives you that specific information.

This relative clause was added to the main sentence, i.e. *the boy is my cousin* using the relative pronoun **who**.

Who is a relative pronoun because it connects a dependent clause in **relation** to the main clause.

Tip

Relative pronouns refer to the nouns that come before them. Nouns placed before relative pronouns are called **antecedents**.

In the above sentence the **relative** pronoun **who** refers to the BOY.

The noun *boy* is called the **antecedent** of the relative pronoun **who.**

Here are some more examples of **relative pronouns** used in different sentences.

1. The new student *who* joined the school badminton team is a state champion.
2. The book *which* I read last week is excellent.
3. The airbus *that* just arrived came from London.
4. This is the man *whose* son received the best player award last week.
5. The student *whom* they selected for the Mathematics Olympiad is from our school.

The pronouns in italics in each of the above sentences are used to link the noun with other words in the sentence.

Pronouns such as *who*, *which*, *that*, *whom*, *whose*, and *what* are *relative pronouns*. Compound words such as *whoever*, *whomsoever*, *whatever*, and *whichever* are also relative pronouns.

Let's Practise

Fill in the blanks with appropriate relative pronouns.

1. All the parents .... were invited, attended the function.
2. The key .... opens this lock is missing.
3. The lady .... car was hit by the bus has informed the police.
4. The girl .... introduced me to you is my sister.
5. The book .... I bought yesterday is lost.
6. The boy .... is the captain of the school team is from my class.
7. The answer .... you gave was wrong.
8. Those students .... work hard always succeed.

Let's Learn

The relative pronoun *whom* is used to refer to the noun that acts as the object of a verb while the relative pronoun *who* is used to refer to the noun that acts as the subject of a verb.

Remember

The relative pronoun *whose* (the possessive form of *who* and *which*) has to be followed by a noun.

This difference is exactly the same as between *he* and *him*, and *they* and *them*. *He* and *they* act as the subjects of verbs, and *him* and *them* as objects.

The difference between the relative pronouns *whoever* and *whomever* is the same.

The relative pronoun *whose* is a possessive pronoun which is used to refer to a possessive noun.

Let's Practise

Complete the following sentences with correct relative pronouns choosing from those given in brackets.

1. Dickens is an author .... (who/whom) I like a lot.
2. .... (Whoever/Whomever) comes first will get the ticket.
3. Everyone .... (who/whom) completed their work can take a break.
4. Your teacher is a person .... (who/whom) you should honour.
5. Guess .... (who/whom) I met in the museum? The President of India!
6. .... (Whoever/Whomever) wants to enrol for the competition should do it by tomorrow.
7. Geeti is the girl .... (who/whom) I know for a long time.

8. .... (Who/Whom) did you speak to when you called my office?
9. The singer .... (who/whom) damaged his vocal cord last year has just announced his comeback.
10. The bakers .... (whom/who) I hired for the wedding canceled at the last minute.
11. .... (Whoever/Whomever) you saw yesterday at the park wasn't me.
12. Alia is my cousin .... (who/whom) lives in New York.

7 Adjectives

Let's Do

The pictures of a few famous monuments are given below. Identify the name of each picture with the help of the list given on the next page.

ICT

1. The *amazing* Great Wall of China
2. The *impressive* Leaning Tower of Pisa
3. The *magnificent* Taj Mahal
4. The *splendid* Roman Colosseum
5. The *majestic* Pyramid of Giza
6. The *enormous* Statue of Christ the Redeemer
7. The *marvellous* Chichen Itza

Remember

An adjective is
- a descriptive word.
- a modifier to a noun.

In the above phrases, words such as *amazing*, *splendid*, *impressive*, *magnificent*, *enormous*, *majestic*, and *marvellous* describe the nouns.

Words that describe a noun are called **adjectives**.

Types of adjectives

The following diagram shows the different types of adjectives.

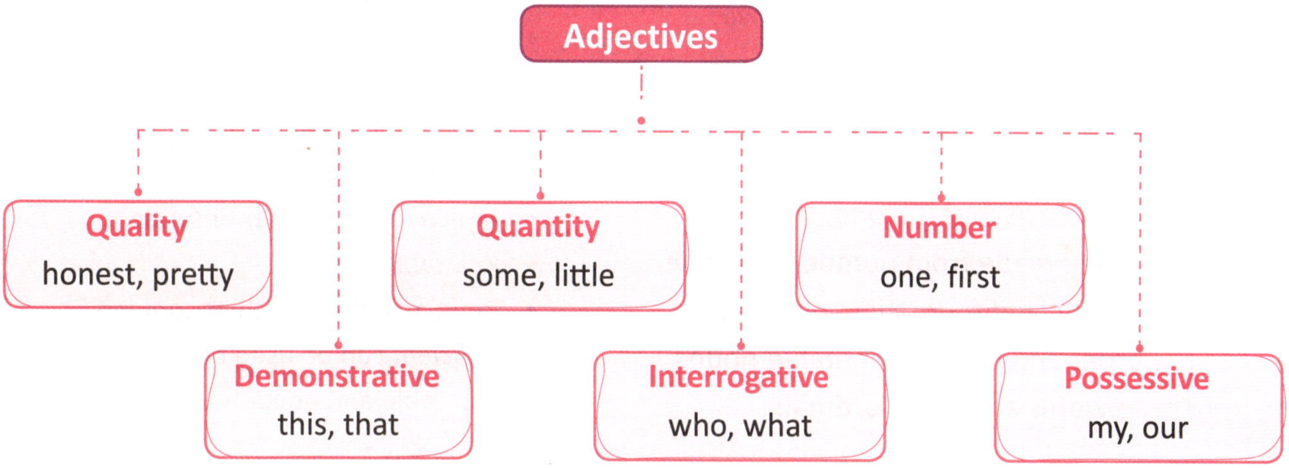

Adjectives of quality

Words such as *majestic*, *amazing*, *splendid*, *magnificent*, *marvellous*, *enormous*, and *impressive* give us information about the quality of the noun. They are called **adjectives of quality**.

If we ask *what kind of* about a noun, the answer we get is an **adjective of quality**.

Adjectives of quantity (quantifier) and number

Read the following passage.

There are *forty* students in Class VI. *Most* students in the class are very obedient. Only *three* or *four* students are very naughty. *Some* girls are very quiet while *a few* boys are very talkative. The teacher gives these boys *enough* work to keep the class quiet. Then they never cause *much* trouble to the teacher and there is very *little* noise. *All* the students love their teacher very much. From the *first* period to the *last* period in school, the students obey their teacher.

Words such as *most*, *some*, *a few*, *enough*, *much*, *a little*, and *all* give us information about the quantity of the noun. They are called **adjectives of quantity**. These *measuring* words modify the noun and are also called **quantifiers**.

Apart from the quantifiers mentioned above, there are other words which denote number.

Examples:

- **Cardinal numbers** such as *one*, *two*, *three*, *four*, and *forty* are used to provide information about the quantity of countable nouns.
- Words such as *first*, *second*, *third*, and *fourth* are made from numbers like *one*, *two*, *three*, and *four*. They tell us about the order and rank of countable nouns. These words are called **ordinals**.

Remember

- *Adjectives of quantity* describe uncountable nouns.
  Example: little patience, much time, enough work
- *Adjectives of number* describe countable nouns.
- Some adjectives such as *some*, *sufficient* can be used both for countable and uncountable nouns.

Cardinal numbers and **ordinals** used to describe the number of countable nouns are called **adjectives of number**.

Let's Practise

Listen the audio on a gymnast from Tripura, Dipa Karmakar who was the first Indian woman athlete to qualify for the Olympics. Identify the adjectives of quality (five), adjectives of quantity (one) and adjectives of number (four), and write them down in the table given on the next page. Replay the audio, if required.

KNOWLEDGE OF INDIA

Adjectives of quality	Adjectives of quantity	Adjectives of number

Let's Learn

Demonstrative, interrogative and possessive adjectives

Read the following letter from a son to his mother.

Dear Mother,

Those books which you sent last Christmas are still lying in *my* home. I don't have time to read them. Ever since I joined *this* office, the work has become very hectic. I remain awfully tired. I need to take *certain* steps so that my work doesn't create *such* tiredness in me. I spoke to my boss about a break. He asked me *what* plans I have for the holiday. I think I'll be able to go and meet you soon after I get *his* permission. Till then...

Yours lovingly,

Amit

- Words such as *those*, *this*, *certain* and *such* point out to nouns such as *books*, *office*, *steps*, and *tiredness*.

> Words which point out to nouns are called **demonstrative adjectives**—*this*, *that*, *these*, *those*, *such*, *certain* and *yonder*.

Words such as *what* are used with nouns such as *plan* to *ask questions*.

> Words which are used with nouns to ask questions are called **interrogative adjectives**—*what*, *which* and *whose*.

Words such as *my* and *his* are used with nouns such as *daughter's home* and *permission* to denote *possession*.

> Words which are used with nouns to denote possession are called **possessive adjectives**—*my*, *your*, *his*, *her*, *its* (singular), *our*, *your*, *their* (plural).

Remember

- Demonstrative adjectives, interrogative adjectives and possessive adjectives can also be used as pronouns.
- They are considered to be adjectives only when they modify a noun.

Let's Practise

Underline the demonstrative, interrogative and possessive adjectives in the following sentences. Write DA next to demonstrative adjectives, IA next to interrogative adjectives and PA next to possessive adjectives.

1. Please pass on this book to Harry. ....
2. Which food do you like the best? ....
3. Whose books are these? ....
4. Is it possible to borrow your laptop? ....
5. Those chocolates were given to me by my aunt. ....
6. Have you seen these comics? ....
7. I met your mom in the market this morning. ....
8. What movies have you seen during this holiday? ....
9. My father is a wonderful storyteller. ....
10. He tells stories in such funny ways that we can't stop laughing. ....

Let's Learn

Making comparison

In English, adjectives can be made from other words by adding suffixes to them.

Look at how some adjectives are formed by adding suffixes to nouns.

Noun	+	Suffix	=	Adjective
1. courage	+	*-ous*	=	courageous
2. faith	+	*-ful*	=	faithful

3. nature + *-al* = natural
4. dirt + *-y* = dirty
5. love + *-able* = lovable

Tip **Suffixes** are a group of letters at the end of a word. **Examples:** *-ful*, *-ous*

Let's Practise

Make adjectives by adding suffixes to the words given in the box. You can use suffixes like: -ous, -ful, -al, -y, -able.

danger	fear	pain	fun	fame	front	joy
study	note	adore	music	enjoy	cure	touch
outrage	air	colour	catch	magic	luck	truth

....

....

....

....

Let's Learn

Making opposites by adding prefixes

We can make opposite words or negative words by adding prefixes to them. *Prefixes* are a group of letters placed at the front of a word.

Examples: *dis-*, *im-*

To get the word opposite in meaning to that of honest,

- we add the prefix *dis-* before the word.
- we get the word *dishonest*.
- the prefix *dis-* in this word denotes *not*.
- the word *dishonest* means *not honest*.

Tip We cannot get the opposites of all words in this way!

There are several other prefixes in English that mean *no* or *not*. Some of them are—*in-*, *un-*, *im-*, *non-*, and *ir-*. We get negative words or words opposite in meaning, if we add these prefixes to different words.

Let's Practise

Make the following adjectives opposite in meaning by adding prefixes to the words given in the box. You can use prefixes like: in-, un-, im-, non- and ir-.

vegetarian	obedient	proper	disciplined	courteous
edible	personal	responsible	relevant	efficient
violence	real	experienced	mortal	rational
organized	seen	resident		

....

....

....

....

Let's Learn

Degrees of comparison

Read the following passage and look at the given picture.

The Sun is surrounded by eight planets in our solar system. The Sun is in the centre with the eight planets travelling around it in elliptical paths.

Planets in the solar system are of different sizes and are at various distances from the Sun. Jupiter is the *biggest* planet. Even Saturn is *smaller* than Jupiter. Mercury is the *smallest* planet.

It is *closest* to the Sun and Neptune is the one *farthest* from the Sun.

In the above passage, words such as *biggest*, *smaller*, *smallest*, give us information about the size of different planets. *Closest*, *farthest*, and *closer* give us information about the distance of different planets from the Sun. These are words which express degrees of comparison among different things.

The three degrees of comparison are as follows.

1. **Positive Degree**—An adjective is in the **positive degree** when there is no comparison and the word is used in its base form to state the quality of the subject.

   Example: Mercury is a *small* planet.

2. **Comparative Degree**—An adjective is in the **comparative degree** when it is used to compare two nouns.

   Example: Mercury is *smaller* than Saturn.

3. **Superlative Degree**—An adjective is in the **superlative degree** when a comparison is made among more than two nouns.

   Example: Mercury is the *smallest* of all the eight planets.

How do adjectives change in form to show comparison?

Generally, we get the comparative and superlative degree forms of an adjective by adding ***-er*** and ***-est*** to its base positive degree form.

Some adjectives are given below with their degrees of comparison.

Positive	Comparative	Superlative
sweet	sweeter	sweetest
bright	brighter	brightest
great	greater	greatest
old	older	oldest
strong	stronger	strongest
dear	dearer	dearest
fast	faster	fastest

Now look at the following forms.

Positive	Comparative	Superlative
large	larger	largest
brave	braver	bravest
fine	finer	finest
wide	wider	widest
able	abler	ablest

Rule 1: Adjectives which end in **-e**, form their comparative and superlative degree forms by the addition of **-r** and **-st**.

Now look at the following forms.

Positive	Comparative	Superlative
pretty	prettier	prettiest
greedy	greedier	greediest
lazy	lazier	laziest
lucky	luckier	luckiest
heavy	heavier	heaviest

Rule 2: For adjectives ending in **-y**, the **-y** is changed into **i** before adding **-er** and **-est** for the comparative and superlative forms.

Look at these forms.

Positive	Comparative	Superlative
hot	hotter	hottest
sad	sadder	saddest
thin	thinner	thinnest
big	bigger	biggest

Rule 3: Sometimes, for adjectives ending in a single consonant such as **t**, **d**, **g**, **n**, etc., the last consonant is doubled before adding **-er** or **-est** to get the comparative and superlative degree forms of the words.

However, remember that there are exceptions to this.

Positive	Comparative	Superlative
broad	broader	broadest
lean	leaner	leanest
short	shorter	shortest
long	longer	longest

Rule 4: Longer adjectives do not take **-er** and **-est** to form their comparative and superlative degree forms. For such adjectives, **more** is used for the comparative degree form and **most** for the superlative degree form.

Positive	Comparative	Superlative
famous	more famous	most famous
beautiful	more beautiful	most beautiful
difficult	more difficult	most difficult

The definite article *the* must be used before the adjective in its superlative degree form.

The comparative and superlative forms of some adjectives are not formed from the positive degree. Here is a list of some irregular forms.

Positive	Comparative	Superlative
good	better	best
bad	worse	worst
far	farther	farthest (for distance)
far	further	farthest (for position)
little	less	least
many	more	most (with countable nouns)
much	more	most (with uncountable nouns)

Let's Practise

1. Read the following passage. Fill in the blanks with the correct forms of adjectives given in brackets. One has been done for you.

When we refer to size, Jupiter is the ....largest......... (large) planet in our solar system. Mercury is the .... (tiny) among all planets. Though Mars is also a .... (small) planet, it is .... (big) than Mercury. Venus is .... (small) than the Earth, but .... (big) than Mars. It is the .... (bright) of all planets. It is because of its brightness that it is called the 'morning star'. Saturn is .... (small) than Jupiter but .... (big) than all other planets. It has .... (many) moons than any other planet. Saturn has as many as 18 moons. Uranus, the seventh planet is .... (large) in size but .... (light) in weight than Neptune. In spite of being .... (small) in size than Uranus, Neptune is .... (heavy) in weight.

2. **Complete the following sentences using appropriate form of the adjective choosing from the three given options. Look at the picture below for clues.**

Nadia, Rohini, and Grace are close friends. They live in the same locality and go to the same school. They love one another very much.

a. Nadia is .... than Rohini.
   i. tall   ii. taller   iii. tallest

b. Grace is the .... among them.
   i. short   ii. shorter   iii. shortest

c. Rohini is .... than Nadia.
   i. short   ii. shorter   iii. shortest

d. Nadia is the .... of them all.
   i. tall   ii. taller   iii. tallest

e. Rohini has very .... hair.
   i. short   ii. shorter   iii. shortest

f. Grace's hair is .... than Nadia.
   i. long   ii. longer   iii. longest

g. Nadia's hair is .... than Rohini.
   i. dark   ii. darker   iii. darkest

h. Grace's hair is the .... of them all.
   i. long   ii. longer   iii. longest

8 The Verb

Let's Learn

A sentence has two parts.

1. The subject which gives information about the doer of the action.
2. The predicate which gives information
   - about the action itself, and
   - sometimes about the influence of the action on someone or something.

Now look at these sentences:

1. I love ice cream.
   - love → verb; ice cream → object (verb + object = predicate)
   - I → subject

2. I gave Mita a book.
   - gave → verb; Mita → object; a book → object (verb + object + object = predicate)
   - I → subject

The predicates in the above sentences have different elements—verbs and objects. The words *love* and *gave* in these sentences indicate action. They are known as verbs.

> The word that refers to an action, a state of being, or possession in a sentence is known as a **verb**.

Love and *gave* are finite **verbs** because they have a tense and a subject with which they agree in number and person.

Now look at the following diagram showing the different types of verbs.

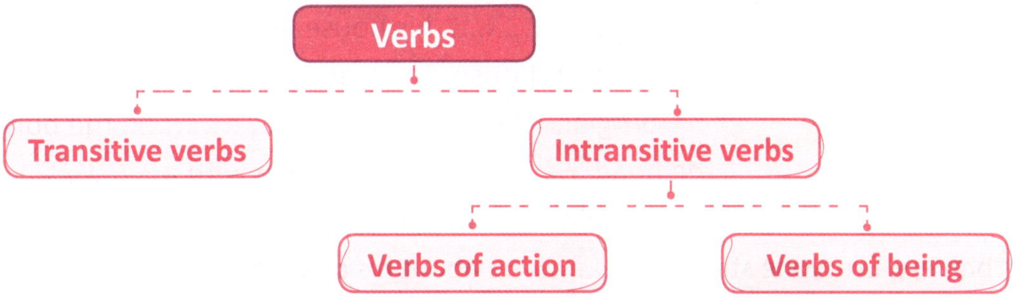

Transitive verbs

In the first sentence,

- the noun *ice cream* completes the meaning of the verb *love*.

- therefore, the noun *ice cream* is the object of the verb *love* in the sentence.

In the second sentence,

- the predicate has the verb *gave*.
- the predicate has the indirect object *Mita*.
- the predicate has the direct object *book*.

The meaning will remain incomplete in the two sentences, without the objects. Objects complete the meaning of the sentence when a particular type of verb is used.

Verbs that must have an object or objects to complete their meaning are called **transitive verbs**.

Since the verbs *love* and *gave* in the two sentences have objects, we can say that they are **transitive verbs**.

Let's Practise

1. Fill in the blanks with suitable verbs or objects from the ones given in the box.

lives	all the valuables	rope	took	hit	a reward
a road	flows	chased	entered	talks	tied

The stream .... down the mountain. Along this stream runs .... Mr Sen .... in a house beside the road. One day, a burglar .... his house. He took .... from his house. The watchman .... the burglar. The watchman .... the burglar on the head. He .... him with a .... He .... him to the police station. The watchman got .... for his bravery. Everyone still .... about his courage.

2. Identify the transitive verbs and their objects in the passage you have just completed and write them down.

3. **Circle the indirect object and underline the direct objects in the following sentences. One has been done for you.**

a. Rani's brother gave (her) a surprise gift on her birthday.

b. The children showed their mother the injured puppy at the corner of their home.

c. Jivesh bought Jinia a cake last week.

d. The English teacher gave us a new assignment.

e. I wish you luck for your project.

f. Please allow me some time to complete the work.

g. Julia made a cup of hot chocolate for her dad.

h. You gave the correct answer to that boy.

i. My granny told us a story.

Let's Learn

Intransitive verbs

Intransitive verbs are verbs that do not take an object.

They are of two types of **intransitive verbs**:

verbs of action (doing), and verbs of being.

Verbs of action

Look at the following sentence.

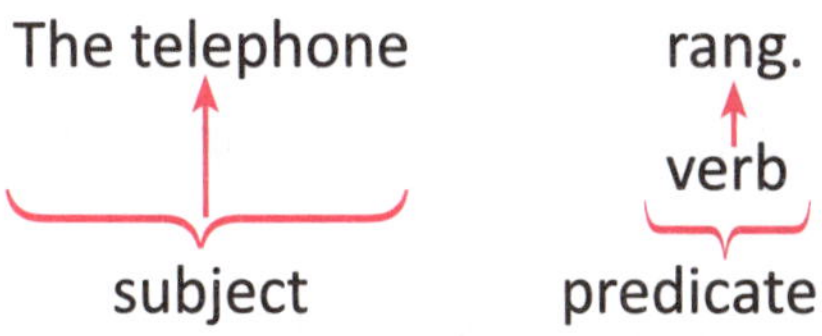

The verb, *rang*, in this sentence

- indicates an action and is called a verb of action (doing).
- is complete in itself, and therefore does not need an object.

Hence, this is an intransitive verb.

Other *verbs of action* such as *smile*, *look*, *die*, *live*, *laugh*, *roar*, and *cry* are examples of intransitive verbs.

Verbs of being

Look at the following sentence.

The lotus | is | the national flower of India.

is ↑ verb; the national flower of India ↑ complement

The lotus: subject; is the national flower of India: predicate

In the above sentence,

- the verb, *is*, expresses a state of being and is called a verb of being.
- the verb, *is*, links the subject, *the lotus*, to the rest of the sentence.
- the complement, *the national flower of India*, refers to the subject, *the lotus*.
- the sentence will be incomplete without the phrase, *the national flower of India*.
- as the phrase *the national flower of India* completes the meaning of the sentence, it is called a **complement**.

Other **verbs of being** such as *are*, *am*, *was*, *were*, *become*, and *became* take complements to make complete sense.

Verbs of being are also known as **incomplete verbs** or **linking verbs**. They are known as linking verbs because they link two parts of a sentence.

Look at the following sentences.

	Subject		Verb		Complement
	Subject	←	**Verb**	→	**Complement**
1.	India	←	is	→	my country.
2.	The leaves	←	became	→	dry.
3.	You	←	seem	→	nice.
4.	Children	←	felt	→	very happy.

- The subject and complement in the sentences given refer to the same person or thing.
- The verb *is* acts as a link between the two in the sentence.
- As the complement refers to the same person or thing as the subject, we call it a subject complement.
- Some verbs of action can also take a complement after the object.

Read the following sentences.

1. The people made him *the leader*.
2. We found him *in a good mood*.
3. The company appointed Ms Rahman *the manager*.
4. I consider her *trustworthy*.

- The words in italics in the sentences are **complements** because without them the sentences would remain incomplete.
- They come after a **transitive verb** + an **object**.
- They refer to the object of the verb and not to the **subject** of the sentence.
- They give us additional information about the **object** in each sentence.
- These **complements** are called **object complements**.

Let's Practise

1. The following sentences contain a subject or object complement. Identify the underlined words in each case as subject complement or object complement.

a. Rani is my friend. ....

b. I find her very smart. ....

c. I met her in school. She became my best friend. ....

d. Rani loves dressing fancy. She recently dyed her hair blue. ....

e. She is also a very good singer and she performs professionally. ....

2. Read the following sentences. Identify the transitive and intransitive verbs.

a. One day Vidyasagar visited an English officer. ....

b. The officer was seated on his chair. ....

c. He had put his booted feet on the table. ....

d. Vidyasagar sat on the chair in front of him. ....

e. The English officer was insolent. ....

f. He didn't put his feet down. ....

g. Vidyasagar was insulted. ....

h. Much later, the officer came to Vidyasagar's office. ....

i. Vidyasagar behaved similarly. ....

j. He taught the officer that everybody needed to be treated with respect. ....

3. Tick the correct answer from the given options about the type of the underlined verbs in each following sentence.

a. I studied all afternoon.

i. linking verb ◯ iii. transitive verb ◯

ii. intransitive verb ◯

b. My brother wrote me an email from the USA.

   i. intransitive verb ◯
   ii. transitive verb ◯
   iii. linking verb ◯

c. My mum was very worried.

   i. verb of action ◯
   ii. linking verb ◯
   iii. transitive verb ◯

d. He seems very happy there.

   i. linking verb ◯
   ii. verb of action ◯
   iii. transitive verb ◯

e. I painted my room yellow.

   i. transitive verb ◯
   ii. linking verb ◯
   iii. intransitive verb ◯

4. Following are some sentences with different types of verbs that you learnt in this chapter. Identify the verb in each of them and complete the table below.

a. Zarina walks to school.
b. Mathews is my cousin.
c. Please open the door.
d. Rani sleeps early.
e. Our neighbours sold their house.
f. My dad's company manufactures jute.
g. Dilip became a well-known writer.
h. The train arrived very late yesterday and I could not go to the city.
i. You must write a letter to me when I'm gone.
j. The book appears to be good.

Linking verb	Transitive verb	Intransitive verb

9 Subject-Verb Agreement

Let's Learn

The agreeing of two or more elements in a sentence is called **agreement**.

Remember

- The number and person of the subject determine the form of the verb to be used in a sentence.
- The number, person and gender of nouns also play an important role in the selection of personal pronouns in the sentence.
- This condition that determines the selection of different words in a sentence is called *agreement*.

This agreement is in relation to:

- number (singular and plural)
- person (first person, second person, and third person)
- gender (masculine, feminine, and neuter)

Read the following sentences.

1. One of the girls in our class is very talented.
2. The students admire her.

In Sentence 1,

- the subject, *one of the girls*, is singular in number and *is*, which is the form of the *be* verb, is also singular.

In Sentence 2,

- the subject, *the students*, is plural in number and the verb, *admire*, is also plural.
- the object, *her*, is a singular feminine personal pronoun.

Subject-verb agreement

There must be an agreement between the verb and the subject in terms of number and person.

- If the subject is singular in number, the verb should also be singular in number.
  Example: Susan *is* playing football.
- If the subject is plural in number, its verb should also be plural in number.
  Example: My parents *are* celebrating their golden wedding anniversary.
- The form of the verb also needs to be modified according to the person of the subject.
  Examples: 1. Sakshi *is* playing in the garden.
  2. Ravi and Rajat *are* working on a project.
  3. Shalu and I *are* baking a pie tomorrow.

Remember

- Main verbs in the simple present tense take an *-s* or *-es* ending when the subject is in the third person singular.
  Example: He loves to paint pictures.
- They remain in their base form when the subject is in the plural.
  Example: They love to paint pictures.
- Auxiliary verbs such as *be*-type and *have*, possess different forms for different number and person.

The following table gives the different forms of the auxiliary verbs *be*, *have* and *do*.

Verb	Person		Number	Present tense	Past tense	Object
be	first	I	singular	am	was	playing.
	second	you		are	were	
	third	she, he, it, Tina		is	was	
	first	we	plural	are	were	studying.
	second	you				
	third	they, Tarun and Tina				

Verb	Person		Number	Present tense	Past tense	Object
have	first	I	singular	have	had	played.
	second	you				
	third	she, he, it, Tina		has		
	first	we	plural	have	had	
	second	you				
	third	they, Tarun and Tina				
do	first	I	singular	do	did	exercises.
	second	you		do	did	
	third	she, he, it, Tina		does	did	
	first	we	plural	do	did	
	second	you				
	third	they, Tarun and Tina				

Let's Practise

Circle the verb given in brackets that agrees with the subject of each sentence.

1. Our cat (is/are) called Minnie.
2. Minnie (is/are) a cute little Burmese cat.
3. She (like/likes) to play with a small tennis ball.
4. I (throw/throws) the ball and Minnie (run/runs) to pick it up.
5. She also (love/loves) to play with my phone.
6. I don't (know/knows) what she (think/thinks) of a phone.
7. But whenever it (is/are) left unattended, Minnie (begin/begins) playing with it.
8. She (keep/keeps) staring at it.
9. It (seem/seems) that sometimes she even (try/tries) to type on it!
10. All my friends (is/are) very fond of her.

Let's Learn

Placement of subjects and verbs

The **subject** comes **before the verb** in a declarative sentence.

- Since there is agreement between the *subject* and the *verb*, they need to be placed close to each other.

  Example: I *love* you.

  (I = subject, *love* = verb, you = object)

In this sentence, the subject is placed immediately before the verb.

- However in some sentences, the subject may not be placed next to the verb. This happens when an entire noun phrase acts as the subject of a sentence. In such cases, the main word of the noun phrase (which is a noun) must agree with the verb.

  Examples: 1. The **story** of my journey *needs* to be told.

  (The story of my journey = noun phrase)

  2. My **students** who admire you very much *want* to meet you.

  (My students who admire you very much = noun phrase)

In sentence 1, the subject, *the story of my journey*, is a phrase.

The highlighted noun *story* is main word in this phrase and is the actual subject of the sentence. The subject is in the third person singular number. Hence, the verb, *needs*, takes an *-s* ending.

Similarly in sentence 2, the subject is a phrase with a relative clause. The main word of this phrase is *students*. It is the subject of this sentence. The subject is in the third person plural number. Hence, the verb, *want*, remains in its base form.

Preparatory subject

Sometimes a sentence begins with the word **there**. In such a sentence, the noun placed after the verb is the actual subject of the sentence, and the word **there** is the preparatory or introductory subject.

Examples: 1. There *was* a lion in a jungle.

2. There *are* ten books on the shelf.

- The actual subject of Sentence 1 is *a lion*; and that of Sentence 2 is *ten books.*
- The actual subject of each sentence is placed after the verb.
- The word *there* used in the sentences is the *preparatory* or *introductory* subject.
- In Sentence 1, the noun *lion* is singular and therefore the verb, *was*, is used.
- In Sentence 2, the noun *ten books* is plural and therefore the verb, *are* is used.

Nouns joined with conjunctions

If two nouns are joined with *as well as*, *with*, or *along with*, the verb agrees with the noun mentioned first.

Examples: 1. The students *along with* the teacher are going for the inter-school competitions.

2. Mrs Avasthi *with* her students *is* also coming for the inter-school competitions.

Of the two nouns *students* and *teacher* in Sentence 1, the first one is in the plural and in the third person. The verb *are* agrees with the noun in number and person. In Sentence 2, the first noun *Mrs Avasthi* is in the singular and the verb *is* agrees with it in number.

Nouns joined with—either ... or, neither ... nor

The verb agrees with the second noun or pronoun when they are joined with *either ... or, neither ... nor* as the subject (nouns/ pronouns).

Examples: 1. *Neither* my friend *nor* I like noodles.

2. *Either* the student *or* the teachers are giving the right information.

In Sentence 1, the personal pronoun *I* is in the first person singular and the verb *like* agrees with it in number and person. Of the two nouns, *the student* and *the teachers* in Sentence 2, the second is in the plural and the verb *are* agrees with it in number.

Let's Practise

1. Fill in the following blanks with appropriate forms of verbs given in brackets. One has been done for you.

a. One of our teachers ....had........ accompanied us to the book fair. (have)

b. Neither Rinku nor her friends .... able to give the answer. (be)

c. Everyone .... happy when each of those problems .... solved. (feel, be)

d. He .... already answered your question. (have)

e. You .... the last one to visit the exhibition. (be)

f. Either you or your friend .... to finish this work. (have)

g. Children along with their parents .... basketball. (play)

h. He .... interesting photographs. (take)

i. Rumi .... me a present last evening. (give)

j. Anu .... a cake every year on her mother's birthday. (bake)

k. Shalini .... a cold today. (have)

2. This is a passage about scuba diving. There are some problems with the verbs in the passage. Read the passage carefully and make corrections in the forms of verb so that the subject and the verb agree in each sentence.

Has you ever heard of a sport called scuba diving? Scuba am the name of an instrument that help a person to breathe while inside the water. It are a sport in which a person can explore the fascinating underwater world of a sea or an ocean. Scuba diving are increasingly becoming a very popular sport among tourists visiting seaside spots. Children of twelve years can starts training for scuba diving. It require training. A person can goes Scuba diving only after taking classes. One need to wear particular dress and uses Scuba equipment for this sport. There is certified trainers who teaches people how to do scuba diving. These lessons can also be taken in a swimming pool.

....

....

....

....

....

....

....

....

....

....

....

....

....

....

....

3. **The following table has three columns. Column A has the subject, column B has the verb, and column C has the object. Match words from these columns to create sentences. Write the sentences in the space given below.**

A	B	C
a. Bittu and Rani	is left	the way to my home.
b. August	have	31 days.
c. An average Indian	begins	more than one language.
d. The function	speaks	at 6 p.m.
e. Neither Riju nor Ghalib	are	a mathematician.
f. Both Junaid and James	is performing	very well.
g. There	is	some jobs that need to be done.
h. German and Sanskrit	has	complex systems of grammar.
i. Babita along with her sister	drive	in Kalabhavan.
j. A little money	know	from my savings.

....

....

....

....

....

....

....

....

....

....

....

....

....

....

10 Verb: Tenses

Let's Learn

Tense is a form of verb which indicates time of an action.

We use

- **simple present tense** to indicate an action that takes place now.
- **simple past tense** to indicate an action that has already taken place before.
- **the future** to indicate an action that is going to take place later.

The table below shows the different forms of the verb for different tenses.

	Simple	Continuous	Perfect
Present	work/works	am / is / are } working	has / have } worked
Past	worked	was / were } working	had } worked
Future	shall / will } work	shall / will } he working	shall / will } have worked

Let's Practise

The verbs in the following sentences are underlined. Identify the tense in each sentence. You can refer to the table given above while doing this exercise.

1. Maya <u>will be going</u> to Sikkim next week. ....
2. The wind <u>is blowing</u> fiercely. ....
3. A villager <u>saved</u> the antelope. ....

4. The bell <u>had rung</u> when I <u>reached</u> the school. ....
5. Shyam <u>lives</u> in Hisar. ....
6. When I <u>was playing</u> in the park, I <u>found</u> a bird's nest. ....

Let's Learn

Tense helps us express an action in terms of **time**.

Tense indicates whether the time of an action is in the **present**, in the **past**, or in the **future**.

Look at the following diagram.

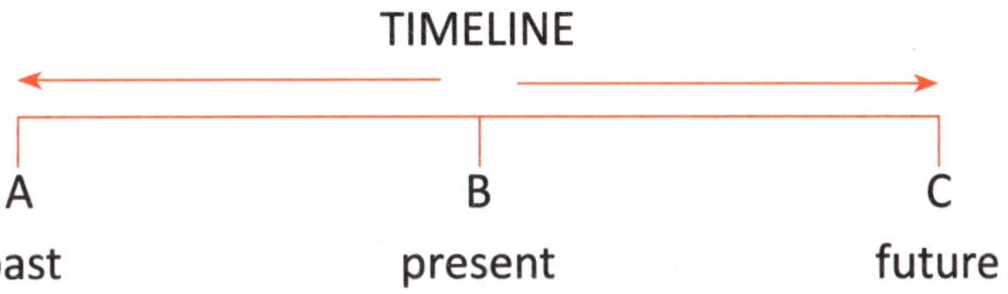

The points, A, B, and C indicate three points in the timeline.

- Point A stands for the time that has already gone (before).
- Point B stands for the present time (now).
- Point C stands for the time yet to come (later).

Remember this timeline. It will help you to understand different tenses in English.

Present tense

Simple present tense

The **simple present tense** can be used in various types of sentences.

- Affirmative sentences

  Examples: 1. She/He sings.
  2. I/We/You/They sing.

- Negative sentences

  Examples: 1. She/He does not sing.
  2. I/We/You/They do not sing.

- Yes/No Questions

  Examples: 1. Does she/he sing?
  2. Do I/we/you/they sing?

- Wh-questions

  Examples: 1. When does she/he sing?

  2. When do I/we/you/they sing?

Let's Practise

1. Choose the correct form of the verb given in brackets to fill in the blanks in the following sentences.

My father .... (help/helps) me with my homework. When my father is not at home, my mother .... (looks/look) after my studies. I also .... (take/takes) help from my brother who .... (study/studies) in class X. There are times when I .... (do/does) my homework on my own. I .... (complete/completes) my homework before I .... (go/goes) to play.

Sometimes my friends .... (come/comes) home and we .... (do/does) our homework together. All of us .... (enjoy/enjoys) working on our Mathematics homework together. My mother .... (give/gives) us merit points if we .... (finish/finishes) our work on time.

Remember

- The verb is used in its base form for the simple present tense with
  - the first person singular and plural—*I* and *we*
  - the second person singular and plural—*you*
  - the third person plural—*they*
- The verb is used in its base form for the simple present tense in
  - negative sentences
  - interrogative sentences
- An *-s* or *-es* is added to the verb in its simple present form when used with the third person singular number—*she/he/it* or any other proper name.

2. Fill in the blanks with the correct forms of the verb given in brackets.

a. My parents .... (like) reading books.

b. The earth .... (revolve) round the sun in 365 days and 6 hours.

c. He .... (go) for a morning walk every day.

d. Sita always .... (complete) her assignments on time.

e. The sun .... (rise) in the east and .... (set) in the west.

f. The Fresh Bakery .... (make) wonderful pastries.

g. A tailor .... (stitch) clothes.

h. Practise .... (make) an individual perfect.

i. Rahul .... (work) very hard.

j. I .... (love) the winter season very much.

k. Julien .... (promise) to take me out for a treat.

Let's Learn

Structure

1. Affirmative sentences

Subject	Verb	Object or complement
I/We/You/They/Ashim and Prerna	watch	television.
She/He/Prerna	watches	television.

2. Negative sentences

Subject	Negative	Verb (base form)	Object or complement
I/We/You/They/Ashim and Prerna	do not	watch	television.
She/He/Prerna	does not	watch	television.

3. Interrogative sentences

Do	Subject	Verb (base form)	Object or complement
Do	I/We/You/They/Ashim and Prerna	watch	television.
Does	She/He/Prerna	watch	television.

4. Wh-questions

Wh- word	Do/does	Subject	Verb (base form)	Object or complement
Why	do	I/you/they/boys	watch	television?
Why	does	she/he/Rani/ Ahmed	watch	television?

Negative and interrogative sentences in the **simple present tense** are formed with the help of the forms of the auxiliary verb *do*.

Let's Practise

Use the words given in the following table and frame five sentences for each of the four types mentioned on the previous page. Use appropriate punctuation marks for each sentence.

Subject	Wh- words	Do verb	Negative	Verbs (base form)	Object or complement
Julie	why	do	do not	study	the gift
we	what	does	does not	live	at home
Adil and Raju	how			begin	our/your/their journey
they	when			finish	his/your/our/ their work on time
I	where			buy	storybooks
you				travel	in/to kolkata
she				want	by train
				read	

....

....

....

....

....

....

....

....

....

....

....

....

Let's Learn

Uses of simple present tense

We use the **simple present tense**:

1. to talk about general or universal truths, that is, to talk about something that was true in the past, is true now, and will be true in the future.

   Examples: a. The sun *rises* in the east.

   b. The earth *goes* round the sun.

2. to talk about routine activities.

   Examples: a. The school assembly *begins* at 9.00 every morning.

   b. We *visit* our grandparents during the winter holidays.

3. to talk about characteristics.

   Examples: a. The cheetah *runs* fast.

   b. Honey *is* sweet.

4. to talk about habits.

   Examples: a. Sarah *drinks* tea without sugar.

   b. Sidhu usually *wakes* up at 5.00 in the morning.

In the examples given above, there is no reference to any definite time. Therefore, in such contexts, the **simple present tense** is known as **present indefinite tense**.

More uses of the simple present tense

1. The simple present is used in exclamatory sentences.

   Examples: a. How fierce the storm *is*!

   b. Here *comes* the villain of the play!

2. The simple present is sometimes used to represent a future action.

   Examples: a. They *leave* for Delhi tomorrow.

   b. Our school *reopens* on Monday.

Let's Practise

1. Fill in the blanks with the correct form of the verbs given in brackets. Mention the function (general truth, universal truth or habit) it plays in each sentence. One has been done for you.

a. The sun ...sets (universal truth)... (set) in the west.

b. My sister .... (draw) beautiful portraits.

c. Water evaporates at different temperatures, but it .... (boil) and turns into vapour at 100°C.

d. Rahul .... (eat) cereals for his breakfast on school days.

e. Mr Avasthy .... (go) for a walk very early in the morning.

f. The sloth .... (walk) very slowly.

g. My parents .... (wake) up early.

h. Water .... (freeze) at 0 degrees Celsius.

i. It .... (rain) heavily during monsoon in India.

j. India .... (celebrate) the Children's day on 14th November.

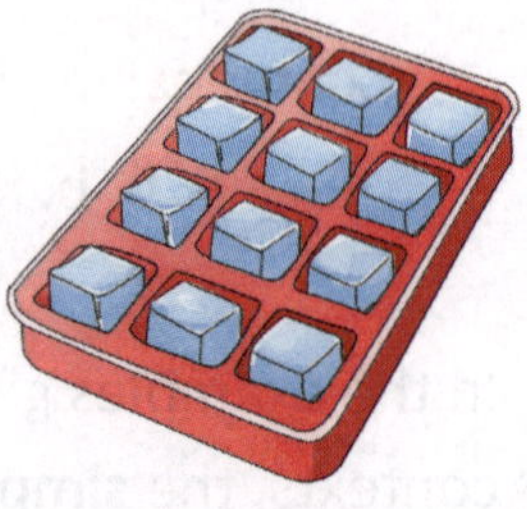

2. **Rewrite the following sentences as directed in brackets.**

a. The school starts at 8:30 a.m. (wh- question)

....

b. I do not like to play cricket. (affirmative sentence)

....

c. Simran completes her homework on time. (negative sentence)

....

d. Anu's friend lives in New Delhi. (yes/no question)

....

e. Does Sunil like to read stories? (affirmative sentence)

....

f. The supermarket closes at 8 p.m. (wh- question)

....

g. I'm not good at singing. (affirmative sentence)

....

h. I want to have chicken soup and bread for dinner. (wh- question)

....

i. Vani is a black belt in Karate. (yes/no question)

....

Let's Learn

Present continuous tense

The **present continuous tense** is used to represent an action that is going on at the time of speaking.

Examples: 1. They *are working* in the kitchen. 2. He *is* still *sleeping*.

Look at the following diagram.

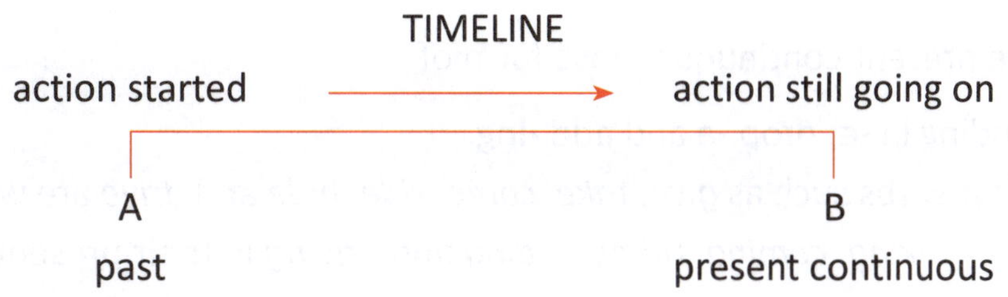

Point A stands for a time in the past and Point B stands for the present. The action started in the past and is still continuing.

Structure

Now look at the following sentences.

1. I *am dancing* now. 2. He *is studying*. 3. The children *are eating* their lunch.

All the above sentences are in the **present continuous tense**. In each sentence, a group of words is used to indicate the continuity of the action in the present—*am dancing, is studying* and *are eating*.

The structure of these words is *am/is/are* + (verb + *-ing*)

Therefore, we can say that the structure of the present continuous tense is as follows:

The present continuous tense = auxiliary (*be*-type) verb + (main verb + *-ing*)

Let's Practise

Fill in the blanks with the present continuous form of the verbs given in brackets.

1. I .... my homework. (do)
2. My mother .... my little sister. (feed)
3. We .... for our annual examinations. (study)
4. The train .... very fast. (go)
5. The children .... in the ground. (play)
6. We .... our lunch now. (eat)
7. Monika and Ulka .... cartoons. (watch)
8. Adil and Sunita .... on their project together. (work)
9. The district hockey team .... new players. (select)
10. My parents .... the house for my birthday. (decorate)

Let's Learn

To make the present continuous tense form of

- verbs ending in **-e**, drop **-e** and add **-ing**.

  Examples: Verbs such as *give, take, come, ride, hide* and *drive* are written as *giving, taking, coming, riding, hiding* and *driving* in their present continuous.

- verbs ending in **-ie**, change **-ie** into -**y**.

  Examples: Verbs such as *lie*, *tie*, and *vie* are written as *lying*, *tying*, and *vying* in their present continuous.

- some verbs ending in **-t**, **-d**, **-g**, **-p**, **-m**, **-n**, **-r**, etc., the last letter is repeated.

  Examples: Verbs such as *cut*, *bid*, *beg*, *sip*, *swim*, *plan*, *stir*, etc., are written as *cutting*, *bidding*, *begging*, *sipping*, *swimming*, *planning*, *stirring* in their present continuous tense.

Let's Practise

Write the present continuous tense of the given verbs.

Base form	Present continuous	Base form	Present continuous
dip		spot	
drive		die	
brag		nod	
hop		bat	
grin		drag	
convince		win	

Let's Learn

Uses of present continuous tense

We use the **present continuous tense**:

1. to indicate an action which is still continuing.

   Examples: a. I *am doing* my homework.

   b. Children *are playing* in the ground.

2. to indicate an action taking place at the present time and not necessarily at the present moment.

   Examples: a. I *am reading* the last book of the Harry Potter series.

   b. He *is studying* medicine.

3. to indicate a future action or event that is pre-determined to happen.

Examples: a. I *am leaving* for Hyderabad tomorrow.

b. Binny *is coming* to Gangtok next month.

Let's Practise

1. Fill in the blanks with the correct forms of the verbs given in brackets. Mention what the tense indicates in each sentence.

a. Rajib .... (expect) a great result in the examinations. ....

b. I .... (go) to school by rickshaw today. ....

c. I .... (learn) classical music. ....

d. The watchman .... (guard) the building. ....

e. My grandparents .... (build) a new house. ....

f. We .... (fly) kites. ....

g. Mohsina .... (participate) in the District Athletics Meet next month. ....

2. Fill in the blanks with appropriate forms of the verbs given in brackets.

a. We generally .... (visit) our grandparents during the winter holidays. But this time we .... (visit) them in the summer holidays.

b. This train usually .... (run) on time. Strangely the train .... (run) extremely late today.

c. It never .... (rain) in October. But this year it .... (rain) even in October!

d. My aunt always .... (knit) beautiful sweaters for all of us. Now she .... (knit) one for me.

e. I .... (go) to school by bicycle every day. But today I .... (go) to school on foot.

f. We .... (plan) a trip to Odisha in August. But it may not .... (happen) because I have my exams.

Let's Learn

Past tense

Simple past tense

We use the **past tense** to indicate an action completed in the past.

Example: I *went* to London.

Here, the verb *went* tells us that the action of going to London took place at some time in the past.

Look at the following diagram.

I went to London.

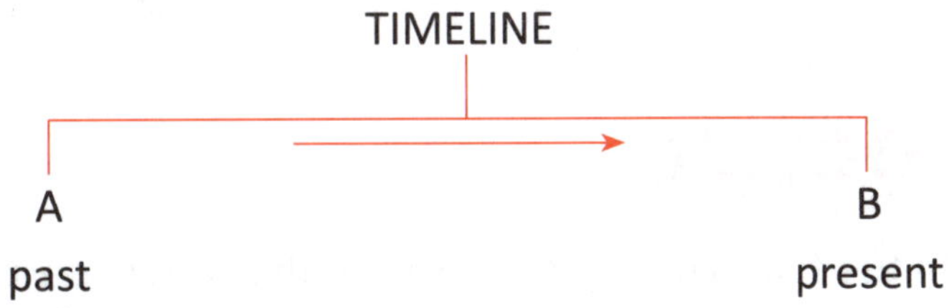

The **simple past tense** can be used in various types of sentences.

1. Affirmative sentences

   Examples: a. She/He sang. b. I/We/You/They sang.

2. Negative sentences

   Examples: a. She/He did not sing. b. I/We/You/They did not sing.

3. Yes/No questions

   Examples: a. Did she/he sing? b. Did I/we/you/they sing?

4. Wh-questions

   Examples: a. When did she/he sing? b. When did I/we/you/they sing?

Structure

1. Affirmative sentences

   subject + simple past tense form of verb

2. Negative sentences

   subject + *did* (past tense form of the auxiliary verb *do*) *not* + base form of verb

3. Interrogative sentences

   a. Past tense form of the auxiliary verb *do* + subject + base form of verb

   b. Wh- question word + past tense form of the auxiliary verb *do* + subject + base form of verb

Uses of simple past tense

We use the **simple past tense**:

1. to talk about a past event.

   Example: I *studied* in Burdwan University.

2. to indicate past habits.

   Example: As a child I always *woke* up early.

3. to narrate a story.

   Example: Once upon a time there *lived* a king.

Let's Practise

Fill in the blanks in the following sentences with the simple past form of verb choosing from the given options.

1. Tanu .... her childhood friend after a long time.

   a. meet b. met c. was meeting

2. The principal .... my application yesterday.

   a. received b. was receiving c. has received

3. My elder brother .... his school last year.

   a. had completed b. completed c. was completing

4. I .... a beautiful film with my mum last weekend.

   a. am watching b. had watched c. watched

5. Vikas .... well for his exams.

   a. wasn't prepared b. didn't prepare c. not prepared

6. Rini .... asleep in the bus.

   a. had fallen b. was falling c. fell

7. We .... our classwork before others.

a. finished   b. was finishing   c. have finished

8. My dad .... the Red Fort when he was in Delhi.

a. visited   b. has visited

c. was visiting

9. Riju .... a novel for his sister.

a. had bought   b. buys

c. bought

10. Ajay .... that he could not play football this week.

a. says   b. said   c. have been saying

Let's Learn

Past continuous tense

The **past continuous tense** is used to indicate an action that started in the past and was going on for some time in the past. In other words, the past continuous tense indicates an ongoing action in the past.

Examples: 1. Grandmother *was watering* the plants when I visited her.

2. Raju and Babu *were waiting* for me at the bus stop for a long time.

Look at the following diagram.

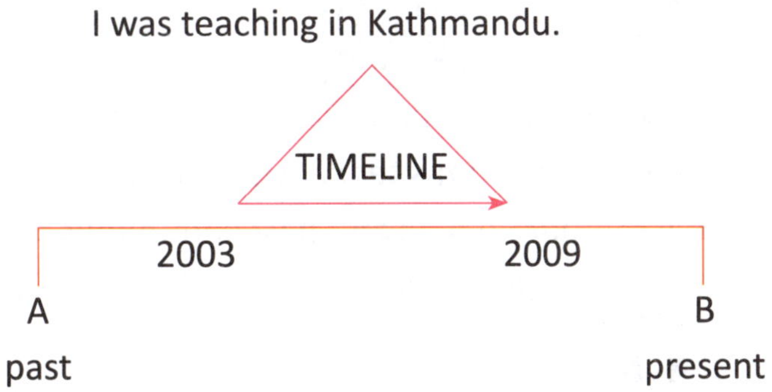

Point A stands for a time in the past and Point B stands for the present. The action started before and was going on for some time in the past.

Structure

Read the following sentences.

1. I *was reading* a book when you came.
2. Simran/He/She *was driving* my car last week.
3. They/You/We *were playing* together without any noise.

All the above sentences are in the **past continuous tense**. In each sentence, a group of words is used to indicate the continuity of the action in the past—*was reading, was driving,* and *were playing.*

The structure of these words is:

was/were + (verb+ *-ing*)

Therefore, we can say that the structure of the past continuous tense is as follows:

The past continuous tense = past form of *be-* verb + (main verb + *-ing*)

Use of past continuous tense

We use the **past continuous tense**:

1. to talk about an ongoing action in a particular period in the past.

   Examples: I *was living* in Hyderabad from 1994 to 1997.
   Jordan was climbing a rock when he broke his leg.

2. to indicate the repetition of an activity during a period of time in the past.

   Examples: Our neighbourhood dogs *were barking* all night.
   Netra was always telling us interesting stories from her experience.

Let's Practise

Listen to the story of Rukhmabai, the first practising woman doctor of India. It is in simple present and present continuous tense. Listen to the story and transcribe (put in written form) it using the simple past and past continuous tense appropriately in the given space. You may have to replay the audio multiple times.

CROSS-CURRICULAR CONNECT | KNOWLEDGE OF INDIA

....

....

....

Let's Learn

The future

Simple future

Simple future tense is when we want to indicate an action that is yet to take place.

There are several grammatical ways of talking about the future.

The most common one is to use modal auxiliaries such as *shall* and *will*.

Look at the following diagram.

TIMELINE

I will visit you tomorrow.

yesterday	now	tomorrow
past	present	future

The sentence in the diagram tells us that 'someone is making a plan of visiting another person the next day.' The time for the visit is *tomorrow*.

Structure

Look at the following sentences.

1. I/We/You/He/She/They *will visit* the museum tomorrow.
2. I/We/You/He/She *shall start* from home at 10 a.m.

The sentences are in the **simple future**. The futurity of the intended action is expressed through the use of modals *will* and *shall*.

In each of these sentences, a group of words is used to express the time of the action *will visit* and *shall start*.

The structure is:

The simple future (affirmative sentences) = modal auxiliary + main verb (base form)

Use of the simple future

We use the **simple future** to:

1. talk about the future.
2. provide information about possible events that have not taken place yet.
3. make a prediction about a future event.
4. discuss some future plans.
5. talk about some definite action expected to take place in the future.

Let's Practise

Change the following sentences from simple present to simple future.

1. This car goes to the airport.

....

2. I plan to finish my homework early today.

....

3. Ali helps poor people.

....

4. This pen writes well.

....

5. The class resumes tomorrow.

....

Let's Learn

Structure of negative and interrogative sentences

We *shall not* start from home before 10 a.m. (negative)

Will you *meet* us at the bus stop? (yes/no question)

When will you *come* home? (wh- question)

All three sentences given above are in the simple future. Their structure is as follows:

The simple future (negative) = modal aux + not + main verb (base form)

The simple future (Yes/No question) = modal aux + subject + main verb (base form)

The simple future (Wh-question) = wh-word + modal aux + subject + main verb (base form)

Let's Practise

Change the form of each sentence given below to the one given in brackets.

1. My grandfather will visit us in the coming week. (wh- question)

....

2. Mosquito bites will cause malaria. (yes/no question)

....

3. She will come to school tomorrow. (negative sentence)

....

4. He will help me with my mathematics homework. (yes/no question)

....

5. I shall be late for the party. (negative sentence)

....

6. They will buy me some nice cookies from the supermarket. (wh- question)

....

Let's Learn

Expressing the future with be- going to form

The **be- going to** form is used to denote:

- an intention

  Example: I *am going to* school now.
- a prediction in relation to future

  Example: You *are going to* be very successful in life.
- the definiteness of some future event on the basis of the circumstances mentioned

  Example: The tortoise *is walking* while the rabbit *is taking* rest. I think the tortoise *is going to* win the race.

The structure of this form is:

form of the *be* verb + *going to*

Let's Practise

Fill in the blanks in the following sentences with will, shall, or be- going to.

1. It .... be very hot this summer.
2. You .... win the elocution competition.
3. We .... move to Delhi soon.
4. The students .... practise for the inter-school football match.
5. Our school .... organize the match this year.
6. The baby bird is opening out its wings. I think it .... fly.
7. The guests won't be staying overnight, ... they?
8. Minnie .... do very well in the competition.

Let's Learn

Perfect tense

Present perfect tense

The **present perfect tense** indicates an action that started in the past and is still connected with the present. The present perfect tense cannot be used if the past action is not connected with the present time in some way.

Look at the following diagram.

TIMELINE

I have known him since 1999.

The sentence in the diagram tells us that— 'I came to know him in 1999 and I still know him.' We use the **present perfect tense** here since the past action of getting to know a person is connected to the speaker's present.

Structure

Read the following sentences.

1. I/We/You/They *have known* him since 2000.
2. Simran/She/He *has eaten* her/his dinner.

The sentences given above are in the *present perfect tense*. In both the sentences, a group of words is used to express the time of the action—*have known, has eaten*.

The structure here is:

the present perfect tense = (the auxiliary verb) *has/have* + the past participle form of the main verb

Use of present perfect tense

We use the present perfect tense:

1. to indicate a finished action that has its impact (result) in the present.

   Example: The policeman *has shot* the terrorist.

2. to refer to an activity or event that occurred in the past.

   Example: *Have you been* to Singapore?

3. to convey news.

   Example: The Prime Minister *has signed* the nuclear deal with the USA.

4. for an action repeated till the present.

   Example: I *have listened* to the song four times since afternoon.

5. to indicate an action that started in the past and is still continuing.

   Example: I *have* always *admired* you.

Remember

The *present perfect tense* generally does not take an adverb of past time – *last week, yesterday*, etc. But it is used with phrases like *so far, since, just, yet, already*, etc.

Let's Practise

1. Make at least ten sentences using the words in the following table. You may not have to use words from all the columns for every sentence.

1	2	3	4	5	6
I We You She He They	has have	already just always	admired prepared received the letter spoken submitted the report mentioned it sent the telegram finished arrived helped	to from in on my	her. him. father. you. the. college. lunch. time.

....

....

....

....

....

....

....

....

....

....

....

....

2. Match the sentences given in column A with the tenses given in column B.

A		B	
a.	Gita told me about it.	i.	present perfect continuous
b.	Raja has never been to Jaipur.	ii.	simple present
c.	I am a vegetarian.	iii.	simple past
d.	Mr Basak has been teaching Maths for the last 10 years.	iv.	present perfect
e.	Ritesh hadn't been paying attention to studies.	v.	past perfect
f.	The principal inaugurated the new building yesterday.	vi.	simple present
g.	I had met your brother before.	vii.	past perfect continuous
h.	Mrs Mukherjee likes my daughter very much.	viii.	simple future
i.	I had already done my shopping for the festival.	ix.	simple future
j.	Ali will receive the guest from the airport tomorrow.	x.	past perfect
k.	The travellers had been walking for five hours.	xi.	past perfect continuous
l.	I shall always remain grateful to my teachers.	xii.	simple past

11 Verb: Voice

Let's Learn

Voice is the property of verbs that tells us whether the *subject* in a sentence actively performs the action, or passively receives/is affected by the action.

Voice is of two kinds:

- active
- passive

Voice

- **Active**: Rita bakes the birthday cake.
- **Passive**: The birthday cake is baked by Rita.

Both sentences above convey the same meaning, though they look different.

In the first sentence, **Rita** is the subject. The verb *bakes* is in the **simple present tense**. As the action is directly done by *Rita*, *Rita* is the **active subject** in this sentence. The verb has an **object**—*the birthday cake*. The first sentence is in **active voice** because the action is directly done by the active subject.

In the second sentence, the **subject** is *the birthday cake*. The verb *baked* is in the **past participle form**. But *the birthday cake* cannot perform the act of *baking* since it is an inanimate object. It is actually the **receiver** of the action *bake*. Therefore, it is the **passive subject** of the sentence. The doer of the action of this sentence is *Rita*.

A sentence in which the subject is passive and receives the action of the verb is in the **passive voice**.

Thus we know that the second sentence is in the **passive voice**. **Active voice** is the form that is used more frequently.

Passive voice—structure

Verb phrase

The verb phrase in the passive voice, for sentences in the present tense comprises:

- forms of the **be** verb—*is, am, are*
- the past participle or the third form of the main verb

Example: write (Active) is written {be (present tense) + (write + en)} (Passive)

NOTE

- Voice is expressed through verbs.
- Passive voice is used when the action is to be emphasized rather than the doer.
- Changing the voice requires changing the structure of the entire sentence.
- A sentence changes from active to passive voice when the subject and object interchange their respective positions.
- Usually, the preposition by is added before the doer of an action in a passive construction.

Let's Practise

Fill in the blanks with the passive forms of verbs given in brackets. All the sentences are in the present tense.

1. We .... music by Mrs Shankar. (teach)
2. Vegetables and fruits .... in this shop. (sell)
3. This school .... by the Rotary Club. (sponsor)
4. This information .... by Hema. (give)
5. The books .... by Rahul. (read)
6. He .... by all. (miss)
7. She .... by your enthusiasm. (encourage)
8. This essay .... by a renowned scholar. (write)

Let's Learn

Personal pronouns in passive construction

Personal pronouns change their forms in the passive voice.

The table below shows how the forms of personal pronouns change.

Active voice	Passive voice
I	me
we	us
he	him
she	her
they	them

Remember
The personal pronoun in the second person *(you)* remains unchanged in both the voices

Agreement

The form of the **be** verb used to form the passive construction must agree with the passive subject of the sentence.

Examples:
1. He takes his dogs for a walk.
2. His dogs are taken for a walk by him.
3. Everyone tells me about this.
4. I am told about this by everyone.

Sentences 2 and 4 given above are the **passive forms** of sentences 1 and 3 respectively.

Since the passive subject is plural in sentence 2, the form of the **be** verb used in this sentence is *are*. Since sentence 4 has a singular, passive subject in the first person, the verb used is *am*.

Tense of the verb

The tense of the active voice remains the same in the passive construction but the forms of the *be* and *have* verbs undergo a change. In the case of the simple tenses (present and past), the auxiliary verb *be* is introduced along with the past participle form of the main verb. In the case of the perfect and progressive (continuous) tenses the forms of the auxiliary verbs *have* and *be* undergo changes.

Look at the following examples:

Active voice	Passive voice
I write a letter. *(simple present)*	A letter is written by me. *(simple present)*
I am writing a letter. *(present continuous)*	A letter is being written by me. *(present continuous)*
I wrote a letter. *(simple past)*	A letter was written by me. *(simple past)*
I was writing a letter. *(past continuous)*	A letter was being written by me. *(past continuous)*
I will write a letter. *(simple future)*	A letter will be written by me. *(simple future)*
I have written a letter. *(present perfect)*	A letter has been written by me. *(present perfect)*
I had written a letter. *(past perfect)*	A letter had been written by me. *(past perfect)*
I will have written a letter. *(future perfect)*	A letter will have been written by me. *(future perfect)*

The following table shows the various structures of the verb phrase for different tenses used in the passive voice.

Tense	Structure	Example
simple present	*am/is/are* + past participle form of the verb	She *is loved* by all.
simple past	*was/were* + past participle form of the verb	We *were looked* after by you.
simple future	*will/shall* + *be* + past participle form of the verb	The test *will be held* today.
present continuous	*am/is/are* + *being* + past participle form of the verb	I *am being forced* to sing.
past continuous	*was/were* + *being* + past participle form of the verb	She *was being forced* to leave.
present perfect	*have/has* + *been* + past participle form of the verb	I *have been told* about this.
past perfect	*had* + *been* + past participle form of the verb	The ticket *had been booked* already.
future perfect	*will/shall* + *have* + *been* + past participle form of the verb	The tickets *will have been booked* by tomorrow.

Note that verbs in the future continuous and perfect continuous cannot be changed into passive voice.

Let's Practise

1. Change the voice of the following sentences from active to passive. Retain the tense of the active voice.

a. Bidhan had addressed the question well.

....

b. Raja has told me about the party.

....

c. The car hit the bus on the highway.

....

....

d. Riti is forcing me to eat the banana.

....

....

e. The police will chase the thief.

....

f. This key can open the door.

....

g. Roma has revised all the chapters for her exam.

....

h. Rani accompanied Zeenat and Riya to the theatre.

....

2. Read the following sentences and write whether they are in the active or passive voice. Then change the voice of each sentence.

a. Senior students organized the school festival last year.

....

b. Students of class IX staged a play.

....

c. The play was written by William Shakespeare.

....

d. The English teacher helped the students in their preparation.

....

e. Student volunteers were being guided by the games teacher.

....

f. The art teacher was giving directions to some students about stage decoration.

....

g. The students had decorated the stage very beautifully.

....

h. The beggar picked up the purse.

....

i. The purse was found by him.

....

Let's Learn

Interrogative sentences

Generally, the rule for the passive construction of interrogative sentences remains the same, though necessary changes take place in the structure of the verb.

Look at the following examples:

Active voice	Passive voice
Did Rishav give up the job?	*Was* the job given up by Rishav?
Have they bought the house?	*Has* the house *been* bought by them?

Let's Practise

1. Change the voice of the following interrogative sentences.

a. Did Oxford University Press publish this book?

....

b. Do a lot of people use mobile phones?

....

c. Did Simran complete the assignment?

....

d. Have all your friends read your poem?

....

e. Have the students of this class set up the stage?

....

f. Did Tina take the gift?

....

2. Change the following sentences first into passive voice and then into interrogative sentences in passive voice.

a. She painted the walls blue.

....

b. We use the pot to bring water.

....

c. She will finish this work by tomorrow.

....

d. Disha is buying vegetables now.

....

e. The students have already read this book.

....

f. Sheela had taken the bag.

....

3. Change the voice of each sentence as directed.

a. A book is being written by me for publication. (active voice)

....

b. Mrs Basu teaches English in Class V. (passive voice)

....

c. The monkey is eating a banana. (passive voice)

....

d. Has my book been returned by you? (active voice)

....

e. I have known your family for the last 30 years. (passive voice)

....

f. The teacher rewarded Vasu for good conduct. (passive voice)

....

g. The report was sent by the journalist in the evening. (active voice)

....

Check Your Progress 2

1. Write the past and past participle forms of the following verbs.

a. arrive	d. doubt	g. hunt	j. rise
b. bring	e. entertain	h. imagine	k. cry
c. cut	f. fight	i. labour	l. open

2. Fill in the blanks so that the subject agrees with the verb in the following sentences.

a. Both my mother and my sister .... in Chennai. (live)

b. Neither this bag nor this book .... to me. (belong)

c. Not only my neighbours but also my best friend .... to be informed. (have)

d. Either Nitin or I .... driving the car. (be)

e. Many persons I know .... eating a healthy diet. (prefer)

f. One of the students .... requested to meet the Officer in charge. (be)

g. Every question in this test paper .... to be answered. (need)

h. Ajit .... reported the theft to the police though the thieves .... caught yet. (have and not have)

i. Everyone from the class .... informed about the competition. (have)

j. You .... requested to take your seats. (be)

3. Rewrite the following sentences as directed.

a. Does Amit go to school by bus? (negative sentence)

....

b. Does Adil travel to Lucknow by train? (affirmative sentence)

....

c. I speak Telugu. (yes/no question)

....

d. Manvi likes western rock music very much. (negative sentence)

....

e. My sister lives in Tripura. (wh- question)

....

f. Isn't Mount Everest located in Nepal? (affirmative sentence)

....

g. Nilesh loves to eat ice cream. (wh- question)

....

h. New Delhi is the capital of India. (yes/no question)

....

i. Steven Spielberg directed the film Jurassic Park. (wh- question)

....

j. I haven't seen the film. (yes/no question)

....

k. Will you be late for lunch? (negative sentence)

....

l. Shahin loves to read novels. (wh- question)

....

m. Aren't this pair of shoes very old? (affirmative sentence)

....

4. Change the voice in the following sentences from active to passive.

a. I have taken some photographs of the event.

....

b. They invited us.

....

c. The society runs this school.

....

d. Will someone receive me at the airport?

....

e. These assignments kept the students busy.

....

f. Students of class VI are decorating the hall.

....

g. Mrs Ghosh is giving them directions.

....

h. I had checked everything.

....

i. She made this poster.

....

j. Are we renovating our house?

....

Test Paper 1

Total marks = 50

1. Choose the correct answer from the options given below. **[5 marks]**

a. Which of the following is not a material noun?

i. water ii. iron iii. book iv. wood

b. The flowers in the .... looked fresh and beautiful.

i. bundle ii. bunch iii. bouquet iv. bevy

c. *Rain* is an example of a .... noun.

i. material ii. collective iii. concrete iv. abstract

d. .... has same singular and plural forms.

i. aircraft ii. goose iii. ox iv. city

e. My uncle's neice is a very good ....

i. hero ii. cricketer iii. lad iv. master

2. Fill in the blanks with a, an, the or X wherever necessary. **[10 marks]**

William Shakespeare was .... famous playwright who lived in England during .... Renaissance. He wrote many .... plays that are still performed today. Shakespeare and his wife, Anne Hathaway, had three children. .... most famous of his plays include Romeo and Juliet, Hamlet, and Macbeth. Do you know that during Shakespeare's time, ... male actors performed all .... roles, including those of women. .... male actors, who played female characters, wore .... dress and spoke in .... high voice. Even though Shakespeare lived hundreds of years ago, his works continue to inspire .... people even today.

3. Fill in the blanks with who, whose, which, or that. **[7 marks]**

The man .... first proved that it was possible to kill disease-causing microorganisms was Alexander Fleming. Fleming was born on a farm .... is in Lochfield in Scotland. He noticed that the wounds of soldiers .... were injured in World War I would not heal easily. He studied the bacteria .... lived in the wounds. In his lab one day he noticed a fuzzy green mould in a dish .... had bacteria in it. This was penicillium. It was penicillium .... led to the development of penicillin. Alexander Fleming is the man .... invention benefitted medical sciences greatly.

4. Fill in the blanks with appropriate adjectives given in the box. **[5 marks]**

large	beautiful	interesting	new	friendly
old	colourful	quiet	delicious	sunny

Last weekend, our family went for a picnic to a (a) .... park. The park was very (b) .... and full of (c) .... flowers and trees. We had our (d) .... picnic lunch under a (e) .... tree. The weather was (f) .... and perfect for outdoor activities. My brother found an (g) .... trail, and we all decided to follow it. As we walked, we met some (h) .... people who told us about a (i) .... spot by a lake. When we reached the lake, we enjoyed the (j) .... scenery and had a great time together.

5. Read the following recipe. Underline the objects and circle the transitive verbs. [5 marks]

Do you want the perfect cake? No cake is good without great frosting! Try this great frosting recipe:

Ingredients:

- 2 sticks of unsalted butter
- ½ cup milk
- 1 teaspoon pure vanilla extract
- 7–9 cups icing sugar

Place the butter, milk, vanilla, and 4 cups of icing sugar in a large bowl. Beat them together with an electric mixer until the mixture is smooth and creamy. Add the remaining sugar gradually until the frosting is as thick as you would like it. Divide the finished frosting into small portions and mix food colours of your choice. You can store it for up to two days at room temperature with a sheet of plastic wrap pressed to its surface.

6. Fill in the blanks with the correct words. **[8 marks]**

a. There is .... umbrella under the table.

b. I .... ready to go to school.

c. The .... of cows are grazing in the field.

d. These berries .... very tangy.

e. .... artwork of Picasso is displayed in the museum.

f. Raman is a very passionate doctor. .... works for 12 hours in a day.

g. .... is your father's name?

h. Shobha .... already cleaned the table.

7. Choose the correct form of verbs to fill in the blanks. [6 marks]

a. I .... reading books before going to sleep.

i. like ii. will like iii. was liking

b. Mrs Bose .... her arm yesterday.

i. has broken ii. broke iii. was breaking

c. Robin .... to Puri next month.

i. has gone ii. will go iii. had gone

d. Ratan .... when we came home for lunch.

i. has cooked ii. had cooked iii. shall cook

e. Akriti .... now.

i. sung ii. was singing iii. shall sing

f. We .... each other since 2012.

i. known ii. have known iii. has known

8. Identify and change the voice of the following sentences. [4 marks]

a. Students from the music club orchestrated a performance.

....

b. The television remote was found by Sumit.

....

c. The play Othello was written by William Shakespeare.

....

d. Raman visited Japan last year.

....

Draw ☺ for Yes, ☹ for No, 😐 for Some of them	To revise these concepts, go to
1. Were you able to identify different types of nouns?	chapters 1, 2 and 3.
2. Could you use the articles correctly?	chapter 4.
3. Could you fill in the blanks with correct pronouns?	chapters 5 and 6.
4. Were you able to use different adjectives appropriately?	chapter 7.
5. Could you identify the transitive verbs and their objects?	chapters 8 and 9.
6. Were you able to fill in the blanks correctly?	chapters 4, 5, 6, 9 and 10.
7. Could you complete the sentences with the correct tenses?	chapter 10.
8. Could you change the voice of the sentences?	chapter 11.

12 Adverbs

Let's Learn

Read the following passage carefully.

> We are standing in front of the *very* beautiful town hall of Kolkata. The town hall was *quite artistically* built *long ago*. It stands *majestically* on Esplanade Row, near the Assembly House. I have *never* seen such a beautiful building.

In the above passage,

- *very* modifies the adjective *beautiful*
- *quite* modifies the adverb *artistically*
- *artistically* modifies the verb *built*
- *long* modifies the adverb *ago*
- *ago* modifies the verb was *built*
- *majestically* modifies the verb *stands*
- *never* modifies the verb *seen*

Very, *quite*, *artistically*, *long*, *ago*, *majestically* and *never* are called **adverbs**.

> An **adverb** is a word that modifies the meaning of a verb, an adjective or another adverb.

Let's Practise

Read the passages given. Underline the adverbs and circle the words they modify.

1. Please read the passage carefully. Read the passage at least twice. Write the correct answers neatly in your notebook. You have to submit your notebook today. Do this exercise silently.

2. Binita looked for her diary everywhere, but she could not find it anywhere. This made her feel extremely sad. She was seldom careless. Where had she kept her diary? She could not concentrate on her studies at all. She was terribly upset.

Let's Learn

Types of adverbs

There are three broad categories of adverbs:

- simple
- interrogative
- relative

The following diagram represents different types of adverbs.

Adverbs

- **Simple**
  - adverbs of place
  - adverbs of manner/ quality
  - adverbs of frequency
  - adverbs of degree/ quantity
  - adverbs of time
  - adverbs of reason
  - adverbs of affirmation or negation
- **Interrogative**
  - time
  - place
  - number
  - manner
  - quantity
  - reason
- **Relative**

Simple adverbs

Adverbs of place

> **Adverbs of place** give us information about the location of an action. They answer the question—*where*?

Examples: 1. Anita looked for Binita *everywhere*.
2. They all went *away*.

In the above sentences, *everywhere* tells us the location of the action 'looking for'. It answers the question, 'Where did Anita look for Binita?'

Similarly, the word *away* tells us the location of the action of 'going'. Such words are called **adverbs of place**.

Adverbs of manner or quality

> **Adverbs of manner or quality** give us information about the way an action is done. They answer the question—*How* or *in what manner* an action is done.

Examples: 1. Sabir managed the whole situation *skilfully*.
2. I was *pleasantly* surprised.

In the above sentences, *skilfully* tells us about the manner in which Sabir managed the whole situation. It answers the question— 'How did Sabir manage the whole situation?' Similarly, *pleasantly* describes the manner of being surprised.

Such words are called **adverbs of manner**.

Let's Practise

Read the following dialogue. Circle the adverbs of place and underline the adverbs of manner.

Amit: Good morning, Renu. Where were you? I was searching for you everywhere. Here is a note from our principal about our new teacher, Miss Sima. Read it carefully.

Renu: Your new teacher, Miss Sima, is coming here this morning. She's a wonderfully gifted teacher. I'm sure you will all like her immensely.

Amit: Let us go and wait for her outside. Miss Sima may not know her way around.

Renu: Look at that lady who is walking fast towards our school. She must be Miss Sima. Amit, could you go there quickly and get her?

Let's Learn

Adverbs of frequency

> **Adverbs of frequency** answer the question—*How often* or *in what order does* an action take place?

Examples: 1. They *seldom* come on time.
2. I met him only *once*.
3. I watch plays *often*.

In the above sentences, *seldom*, *once* and *often* give us information about the frequency (rate of occurrence) of a particular action. Such words are called **adverbs of frequency**.

Adverbs of degree or quantity

> **Adverbs of degree or quantity** offer information regarding the degree or extent of an action. They answer the question—*How much* or *in what degree* or *to what extent*?

Examples: 1. They were *fully* prepared.
2. He was *rather* busy at the time.

Let's Practise

Fill in the blanks in the following sentences with appropriate adverbs from those given in the box. The type of adverb is given in brackets.

wholly	finally	fast	partially	thrice	really	loudly	hardly
anywhere	safely	initially	rather	once	thoroughly	quickly	inside

I was .... (adverb of degree) aware of the danger when I entered the burning train. All that I thought at that moment was to bring the girl out of the fire .... (adverb of manner). I tried entering the compartment through the emergency window

.... (adverb of frequency) and ....

(adverb of frequency) through the half open door. It was .... (adverb of degree) difficult because the train was running .... (adverb of manner). I jumped into the compartment through the door. .... (adverb of frequency), I could not find the girl .... (adverb of place). I called out for her .... (adverb of manner). There was no one .... (adverb of place). .... (adverb of frequency), I found her behind a sack full of sugar. She was .... (adverb of degree) conscious. She could .... (adverb of degree) keep her eyes open. I shook her .... (adverb of degree) to wake her up. The fire was becoming .... (adverb of manner) bad. I held her tight and .... (adverb of manner) jumped out of the train.

Let's Learn

Adverbs of time

Adverbs of time provide information about the time of occurrence of an action. They answer the question—*When*?

Examples: 1. I shall go there *tomorrow*.

2. They *never* turned up.

Words such as *today*, *tomorrow*, *yesterday*, *never*, *ever*, *sometime*, *now*, *then*, *soon*, *early*, *later*, and *late* are examples of **adverbs of time**.

Adverbs of reason

Adverbs of reason logically connect the conclusion with the argument made in previous sentences.

Examples: 1. *Therefore*, nothing could be done regarding the matter.

2. *Hence*, I am unable to help you.

Words such as *therefore*, *hence*, *however*, and *nevertheless* are examples of **adverbs of reason**.

Adverbs of affirmation or negation

Adverbs of affirmation or negation are used to confirm or negate an action.

Examples: 1. He will *certainly* meet you at the station.

2. I shall *definitely* go on a holiday at that time.

3. I do *not* want to go.

Words such as *yes*, *indeed*, *surely*, *certainly*, *undoubtedly*, and *definitely* are examples of **adverbs of affirmation**. Words such as *no*, *not*, and *never* are examples of **adverbs of negation**.

Let's Practise

Read the following sentences and underline the adverbs of time, reason and affirmation or negation. Write the type next to each sentence.

1. Nowadays the weather is pleasant. ....
2. I was stuck in a traffic jam. Hence, the delay. ....
3. I was about to go out and it started raining then. ....
4. Do your homework now. ....
5. I'll definitely come to your house for the party. ....
6. Binita is not good at football. Therefore, we cannot take her into the team. ....
7. My father will come back from his trip soon. ....
8. India will certainly pay more attention to athletics for the next Olympics. ....
9. My birthday party is tomorrow. ....
10. The district women's cricket team is definitely going to win the trophy. ....
11. Vikram is never late for meetings. ....

Let's Learn

Interrogative adverbs

Words such as *when*, *how*, *where*, *why*, *how often*, and *how long* are used for asking questions. These are known *as* **interrogative adverbs**. Such adverbs are used to ask questions about *time*, *place*, *manner*, and *reason*.

Examples:

1. Time: *When* will you go to London? How long will you stay there?
2. Place: *Where* has Jonathan come from?
3. Manner: *How* did she go to the party?
4. Reason: *Why* do you wish to re-examine the script?

Relative adverbs

Adverbs that modify a word and refer back to an antecedent are known as **relative adverbs**. Words such as *when*, *where*, and *why* are examples of relative adverbs.

Look at the following sentences.

1. He could not recognize the place *where* we used to play.
2. I cannot remember the day *when* I last saw a movie.

Tip

Antecedent is a thing or a person that the pronoun refers to.

In sentence 1, the relative adverb *where* refers back to the antecedent, *the place* and modifies it. Similarly, in sentence 2, the relative adverb *when* refers back to the antecedent, *the day* and modifies it.

Let's Practise

1. Fill in the blanks in the following sentences with the type of adverb given in brackets.

a. .... (interrogative adverb of time) was this school established?

b. I remember the time .... (relative adverb) I first visited the zoo.

c. .... (interrogative adverb of number) students are there in your class?

d. .... (interrogative adverb of reason) did you choose to study art?

e. .... (interrogative adverb of place) do you come from?

f. .... (interrogative adverb of manner) are you planning to come to the party?

g. I don't remember .... (relative adverb) I reached the library on that day.

h. Payal forgot .... (relative adverb) she lost her purse.

i. Could you please tell me .... (interrogative adverb of quantity) flour will I need for the cake?

j. .... (interrogative adverb of frequency) do you eat fast food?

2. Complete the following sentences choosing the correct adverb from the given options in the box below. You can use one adverb more than once. After you have completed the sentence, write the type of the adverb you chose.

how	when	why	never	mostly	very	however
last week	inside	usually	efficiently	positively	well	how much

a. Bittu's friends .... play football.

b. Teach me .... to bake a cake.

c. You'll not understand .... I care for you.

d. I .... study at night.

e. The students of the C section of the Class VI have .... organized the assembly this week.

f. Everyone in school was .... impressed with the programme.

g. .... we had a unit test.

h. This bus will .... reach on time.

i. It is very warm ....

j. .... does your school begin?

k. Please tell me .... are you so angry.

l. You drive so ....

m. .... are you doing?

n. I don't see your point. ...., I'll try to help you.

o. Raja will .... come to see me this week.

Let's Learn

How do we form adverbs?

Most adverbs of manner end with **-ly**. In fact, such adverbs are formed by adding **-ly** to some other words. We can form adverbs by adding *-ly* to adjectives.

Examples:

obvious + *-ly* = obviously
(adjective) (adverb)

Remember

- Words ending in *-le* change to *-ly*.
  Examples: *simple–simply; possible–possibly*
- Words ending in *-y*, change the *-y* into an *-i* when *-ly* is added to them to form an adverb.
  Examples: *heavy–heavily; merry–merrily*
- Most words ending in *-l*, simply add the *-ly* in their adverbial forms.
  Examples: *general–generally; usual–usually*

Let's Practise

Make adverbs from the following words. Then make sentences with the adverbs.

1. warm	3. bold	5. poor	7. steady
2. charming	4. polite	6. hasty	8. certain

....

....

....

....

....

....

....

....

Let's Learn

Comparison of adverbs

Like adjectives, adverbs can also be used in the positive, comparative and superlative degrees.

Look at the following examples.

1. Ajit can run *fast*.
2. Anil can run *faster* than Ajit.
3. But Shireen can run the *fastest*.

Shorter adverbs with one syllable and sometimes with two syllables, make the **comparative** and **superlative** degrees by adding **-er** (2) and **-est** (3) to the positive form.

Adverbs ending in **-ly** take **more** and **most**, and **less** and **least** (to indicate negative meaning) (with the positive forms) to indicate the **comparative** and **superlative** degrees.

Look at the following examples.

1. Please say it *clearly*. Avani has said it *more clearly* and Ravi *most clearly*.
2. Please don't talk so *loudly*. You should talk *less loudly* in the class and *least loudly* when you are in the school assembly.

The following is a list of such adverbs in the three forms.

Positive	Comparative	Superlative
easy	easier	easiest
early	earlier	earliest
fast	faster	fastest
high	higher	highest
loud	louder	loudest
near	nearer	nearest
slow	slower	slowest
soon	sooner	soonest

Some adverbs have irregular ways of forming the comparative and superlative degrees.

The following is a list of such irregular adverbs in the three forms.

Positive	Comparative	Superlative
far	farther/further	farthest/furthest
bad	worse	worst
late	later	last
little	less	least
much	more	most
good	better	best

Let's Practise

Fill in the blanks with the positive, comparative, and superlative degrees of adverbs given in brackets.

1. Could you please talk ....? Anisha talks .... than Piu. Sara speaks .... than anybody else. (softly)
2. Ajay ran .... and Imtiaz ran .... But George won the medal as he ran the .... (fast)
3. They say I sing .... But Mita sings .... than I do. And you must listen to Nitu. She sings the .... of all. (well)
4. I don't like to watch programmes on TV .... My sister dislikes it even .... and my father dislikes it the .... (much)
5. Rimi is .... to go to the party. But it is .... that Diya would go as she loves such parties. And it is .... that Deepa would go as the host is her best friend. (likely)
6. Jia's phone rings quite .... Everyone thought that it was a phone with the loudest sound in the entire class. We thought so till Bubai's phone rang. It rung .... than Jia's. (loudly)
7. I have been living in a hostel for the last three years. I miss my parents. I .... call both to chat. But I chat with my mother .... than I chat with my father. (often)

8. The price of properties had gone .... in urban areas. But the price of property got .... in metro cities. (high)
9. Last Diwali we made candles at home. They were burning .... My dad said that they were burning .... than the ones that he bought from the shop. I felt so happy. (brightly)

Let's Learn

Position of adverbs

There are three positions of adverbs in a clause or sentence. They can be placed

- at the beginning
- in the middle
- at the end

Read the following sentences.

1. *Tomorrow* we have our games class. (adverb at the beginning)
2. I can *hardly* believe my eyes. (adverb in the middle)
3. I met my teacher *yesterday*. (adverb at the end)

Structure

1. **Verb + Adverb**

   When the verb does not have an object or complement, place the adverb immediately after it.

   a. She works *hard*.

   b. Amit runs *fast*.

2. **Verb + Object + Adverb**

   When the verb has an object or complement, place the adverb immediately after the object.

   a. He gave his reply *immediately*.

   b. She answered the questions *satisfactorily*.

3. **Adverb + Verb**

   Adverbs of time like *always*, *before*, *never*, *often*, and *seldom* are placed before the verb.

   a. He *seldom* makes a mistake.

   b. We *always* try to help him.

4. **Auxiliary Verb + Adverb + Main Verb**

When the verb consists of a helping verb and a principal verb, the adverb is placed between the two.

a. He was *greatly* praised for his conduct.

b. I had *completely* forgotten about my test.

5. **Adverb + Adjective—as in the first sentence**

Adverb + Adverb—as in the second sentence

An adverb is placed before an adjective or another adverb which it modifies.

a. You are *absolutely* right.

b. Get my bag *very* quickly.

Let's Practise

Choosing from the box below, insert the adverb into each of the following sentences in its correct position. There can be more than one right answer.

briefly	probably	hardly	never
always	completely	quite	almost

1. We speak in English in class.
2. The food is ready.
3. It will rain tonight.
4. I agree with you.
5. What you say can be true.
6. The thunder in the clouds is loud.
7. Whenever I lend someone a book, it may come back.
8. I like watching films on my own.
9. The principal spoke to us.

13 Prepositions

Let's Learn

Prepositions are very important structural words in English. Structural words are words that help in building the grammatical structure of the sentence.

A **preposition** is a word which is usually placed before a noun or a pronoun and indicates the connection between two or more words.

Read the following passage.

The Taj Mahal is one *of* the most famous buildings *of* the world.

It is one *among* the World Heritage sites declared *by* the UNESCO and one *of* the seven wonders *of* the world.

The building work started *in* 1631 *under* the patronage *of* the Mughal emperor Shah Jahan and ended *in* 1654.

Though it is known *by* the name *of* the emperor, nearly 22,000 labourers, including several architects, led *by* Ustad Isa *from* Persia, created the Taj.

In the above passage, words such as *of*, *among*, *by*, *in*, *under*, and *from* help building the sentences by joining different words and phrases. For example:

- The first *of* in the first sentence, is placed before the noun phrase 'the most famous buildings of the world'. It joins the word *one* to the noun phrase. It tells us that there are many famous buildings in the world and the Taj is one of them.
- *Among* in the second sentence, tells us about the position of this building in relation to other famous buildings of the world.
- *In* in the third sentence placed before the date, tell us about the period of time that was used for the action *of building.*
- *Under* (placed before 'the patronage') and *of* (placed before 'the Mughal emperor Shah Jahan') in the third sentence tell us about the people who planned, funded and executed the work.

- *By* (placed before Ustad Isa) and *from* (placed before Persia) in the fourth sentence tell us about the name and the place of origin of the architect of this magnificent building.

Of, *among*, *by*, *in*, *under*, and *from* link different words in each sentence in the passage.

Such words are called **prepositions**. The word **preposition** means **positioned before** or **placed before** (**pre**—means before) another word.

Let's Practise

Underline the prepositions in the following sentences.

1. Identify the preposition in this sentence.
2. This will take just a minute of your time.
3. Your teacher will discuss the answers after you finish your work.
4. A preposition is usually placed before a noun or a pronoun.
5. It indicates the relation between two or more words.
6. In some sentences, the preposition is placed after the word it modifies.
7. Prepositions are very important in the formation of English sentences.
8. In this chapter you will learn more about different prepositions.
9. There are different types of prepositions.
10. There are prepositions of place, of time and of direction that you need to learn.

Let's Learn

Types of prepositions

There are various types of prepositions.

The following diagram shows the prepositions of place, time, and direction.

Prepositions

Place	Time	Direction
in, at, on, above, between, below, over, across	at, on, in, by, until, till, during, for	to, into, towards, onwards, onto, through, along, over

Prepositions of place

Read the following sentences.

1. The teacher is still *in* the classroom.
2. Our shop is located *at* the corner of the street.
3. Jatin and Rizwan met *on* a bus.

Prepositions such as *in*, *at*, and *on*, in the above sentences, tell us about the location of the teacher, the shop, and the meeting place of Jatin and Rizwan.

Since these prepositions *in*, *at* and *on* give us information about place or location, they are called **prepositions of place**.

The following chart shows some prepositions of place and their meaning.

<table>
<tr><th>Preposition</th><th></th></tr>
<tr><td>in
(used to mean the location of a thing or a person inside a limited area, room, building, or country)
Example: The ball is in the box.</td><td>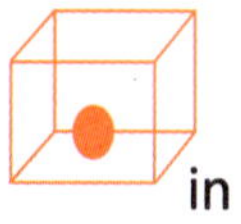
</td></tr>
<tr><td>at
(used to indicate a particular point, meeting place, etc.)
Examples: The ball is at the centre of the circle.
I'll meet you at the shop.</td><td>
</td></tr>
<tr><td>on
(used for a point on a line or surface, public transport, etc.)
Examples: The box is on the way.
The box is on the table.</td><td>
</td></tr>
<tr><td>above
(used to mean at a level higher than something)
Example: The orange ball is above the white ball.</td><td>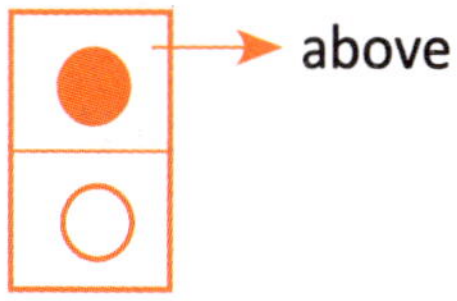
</td></tr>
<tr><td>under
(used to mean below something)
Example: The ball is under the box.</td><td>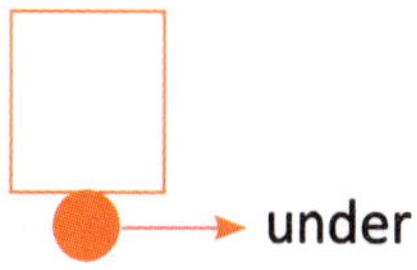
</td></tr>
</table>

Preposition

below

(used to mean at a level **lower than** something)

Example: The white ball is *below* the orange ball.

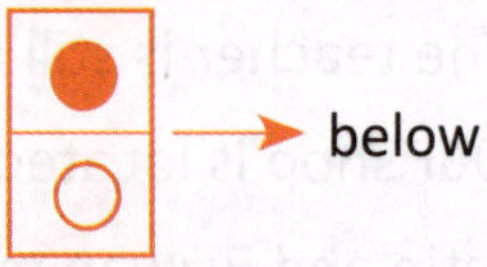

by

(used to mean **next to**)

Example: The ball is placed *by* the box.

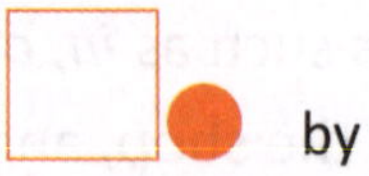

beside

(used to mean **next to** or **at the side of**)

Example: The pool is *beside* the road.

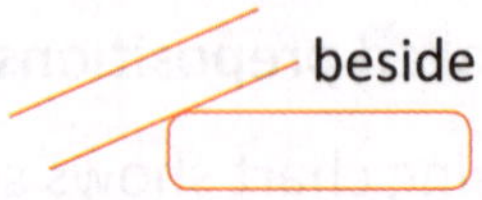

between

(used to talk about **two persons, places, things**)

Example: The ball is *between* the two boxes.

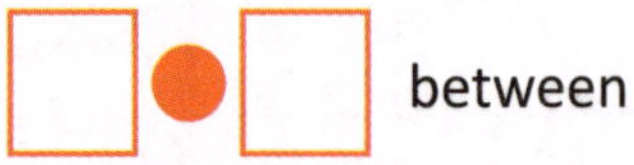

among

(used to talk about **many persons, places, things**)

Example: The orange box is kept *among* the white boxes.

behind

(used to talk about a **position that is partly or fully covered by something in front**)

Example: Ajit is walking *behind* Amit.

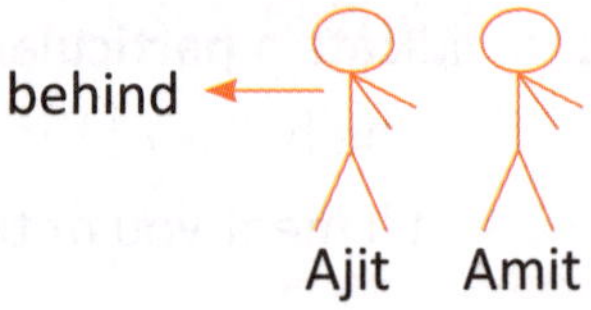

Let's Practise

Make sentences with the prepositions given below.

1. inside:

....

2. between:

....

3. beside:

....

4. above:

....

5. under:

....

6. next to:

....

7. around:

....

8. outside:

....

9. on:

....

10. at:

....

11. by:

....

12. among:

....

Let's Learn

Prepositions of time

Prepositions such as *at*, *in*, and *on* indicate time. They are known as **prepositions of time**.

Read this sentence.

Rita will meet Mita *at* 7 a.m. *at* the bus stop.

Here, the preposition *at* is used twice.

Each time it plays a different role:

- at 7 a.m.: here, *at* helps us know what time Rita is going to meet Mita.
- at the bus stop: here, *at* tells us about the place where they are going to meet.

Therefore, we can say that the first *at* in this sentence is a preposition of time and the second is a preposition of place.

Here is a list of some more **prepositions of time**.

Preposition	What it indicates
at	• particular time of the day **Example:** *at* 7 a.m. • particular point of time **Example:** *at* the beginning of the school year • festivals **Examples:** *at* Onam, *at* Lohri, *at* New Year's

Remember

At is also used in the following expressions:
at first, at the beginning, at the end, at last, at times, at once, at the moment, at present

Preposition	What it indicates
on	• dates **Example:** *on* the 25th of December • days **Example:** *on* Monday
in	• entire period of time **Examples:** *in* this century, *in* the 19th century, *in* ancient times • part of a period of time **Examples:** *in* summer, *in* the morning
by	• a time limit **Example:** Rita will meet Mita *by* 7 in the morning. (Here the time limit is till 7 a.m.)
until	• a time limit (continuation of an action) **Example:** I'll study *until* dark. (This means that I'm studying now and I'll continue my studies till it is dark in the evening—so evening is the time limit here.)
for	• the length of an action or how long an action lasts **Example:** Rita walks *for* an hour every morning.
during	• duration of an action **Example:** I study *during* the night. • known period of time **Example:** I visited my grandparents *during* the holidays.

Preposition	What it indicates
between	• the duration between two points of time Example: I'm available *between* 5:30 and 6 in the evening.
within	• before the end of a certain period Example: The work should be done *within* three days.

Let's Practise

1. **Fill in the blanks with suitable prepositions. You must use the prepositions of time given above and on the previous page.**

Dear Mom,

How are you? We reached Aizwal .... 5 p.m. .... the evening. .... the moment we are staying in a Tourist Lodge on Mall Road. The Tourist Lodge follows a very strict schedule. The morning tea is served .... 6:30 a.m. sharp. We have to eat our breakfast .... 8 a.m. after which the dining hall is closed. Lunch is served .... 1 p.m. and 2 p.m. and evening tea is available only .... 6:30 p.m. and not after that. We must go for dinner .... 9 p.m. or else we will have to eat out.

I enjoy my stay here. We go for a walk .... the morning. .... the day, we visit different places of tourist interest here. Yesterday we were so tired that we slept .... two hours .... the afternoon! .... the evening we watch TV .... it's time for dinner.

When I reach home .... the 14th, I'll tell you more about our stay. I miss you mom.

Yours affectionately,

Jhilmil

2. **Fill in the blanks of the following passage with appropriate prepositions selecting from the ones given in the box below. You can use a preposition more than once.** KNOWLEDGE OF INDIA

of	for	by	during	in	on

Pandita Ramabai was a reputed Indian social reformer, a champion .... women empowerment, an advocate .... women's education as well as removal .... the custom .... child marriage, and a Sanskrit scholar. She was born .... Karnataka .... 23 April in 1858. .... 1878 she became well known throughout the country .... her scholarship .... Sanskrit. She was invited .... the University .... Calcutta (now Kolkata) .... 1878 to deliver lectures in Calcutta. The university gave her the title .... Pandita .... recognition .... her knowledge and scholarship. She married a Bengali from Calcutta .... 1880. .... a brief stay .... two years .... Calcutta, she along with her husband planned to begin a school .... child widows in Calcutta. But that plan could not be realized as her husband died .... 1882. After her husband's death, she moved to live .... Pune and established Arya Mahila Samaj.

Let's Learn

Prepositions of direction

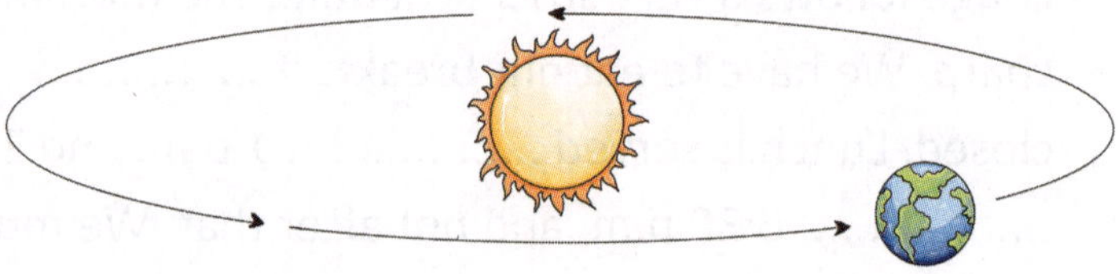

Look at the following sentences.

1. I'm going *to* school now.
2. The earth goes *round* the sun.
3. The army is heading *towards* Kargil.

Prepositions such as *to*, *round*, and *towards* give information about the direction or movement of persons or things. These prepositions are known as **prepositions of direction**.

The following list gives some **prepositions of direction** with examples.

Preposition	What it indicates
to	• direction **Example:** I am going *to* school now.
into	• directions or destinations **Example:** The boy walks *into* the class.
towards	• a specific direction **Example:** The boy is walking *towards* the school.

Preposition	What it indicates
onto	• to express movement on a particular place **Example:** How did the lion get *onto* the roof?
along	• parallel movement or a side by side movement **Example:** I'm walking *along* the river.
through	• a movement in a three-dimensional space, a room, a building **Example:** I walked *through* the room.
across	• a movement towards another side of a flat surface **Example:** Go *across* the road.
over	• a movement ▪ towards the other side of an uneven or higher surface ▪ covering an area **Examples:** The boy climbed *over* the wall. He is known all *over* the world.

Let's Practise

1. Underline the prepositions of direction in the following passage.

Shobhita: Could you please tell me the way to the library?

The receptionist: After you are out of the building, turn right and walk along. At the end of the road, turn towards your left. Go across the road from the traffic light. Walk along the footpath till you reach the post office. From the post office take the lane to your left. Go past the supermarket and walk towards east till you reach the petrol booth next to a children's park. Go through the park. You'll reach the MG Road. Keep walking along to your right for about five minutes. You'll be able to see the grey building to your right.

2. Complete each of the following sentences with the correct preposition selecting from the given options.

a. My English class starts (at/in/on) 10 a.m.
b. Bodhi forgot his school diary (at/in/into) home.
c. The class teacher sent a note (from/to/at) his parents.
d. Idris always listens to the news (from/before/ in) going to sleep.

e. I walk (from/to/with) Imran (at/in/to) school.

f. Mrs Sen has been a teacher (by/for/from) twenty years.

g. You should return my book (by/for/in) next week.

h. You should walk (by/through/along) the footpath.

i. My house is (in/on/across) the road.

j. Walk (at/on/into) the office and ask (in/on/for) some chalks.

Let's Learn

Position of prepositions

Although a preposition is usually placed before (*pre*—means before) a noun or pronoun, sometimes it comes after the word which it modifies.

- The preposition always comes at the end of the sentence when its object is the relative pronoun, *that*.

  Examples: 1. Here is the bag *that* you were looking *for*.

  2. This is the novel *that* I am very fond *of*.

- The preposition usually comes at the end, when its object is an interrogative pronoun.

  Examples: 1. What are you talking *about*?

  2. Whom are you thinking *of*?

- The preposition comes at the end, when its object is a relative pronoun, understood and not stated.

  Examples: 1. This is the book I was speaking *of*.

  2. There is the friend I was referring *to*.

Let's Practise

Fill in the blanks with appropriate prepositions.

1. This is the kind of music that I love to listen ....
2. We are waiting .... the station .... the last three hours.
3. The bridge .... the river was broken.
4. I dream .... becoming a doctor one day.
5. This is the film I was referring ....
6. What are you looking .... ?
7. I'm looking .... a red T-shirt.

Let's Learn

Objects of prepositions

Words which come after a preposition are called **objects of prepositions**.

Read the following sentences.

1. I'm looking *at your haircut*.
2. I was referring *to this film*.

In sentence 1 *your haircut* is the object of the preposition *at*.
In sentence 2, *this film* is the object of the preposition *to*. Most prepositions need an object to complete their meaning.

Let's Practise

Underline the prepositions and circle their objects in the following sentences.

1. I love to listen to western music.
2. We are waiting at the station.
3. The dog jumped over the fence.
4. I am watching birds flying in the sky.
5. Show your answers to your teacher.
6. This aircraft flies to Delhi.
7. The cat got onto the roof easily.
8. I'm so angry with you.
9. The boss cannot meet anyone before afternoon.
10. The school team played well in the match.

Let's Learn

Group prepositions

Besides single-word prepositions such as *on*, *in*, *about*, *above*, *outside*, *underneath*, etc., there are some groups of words that function as prepositions.

Examples:

in spite of	owing to	instead of	on behalf of
in front of	due to	for the sake of	in the course of
by means of	as a result of		

Let's Practise

Fill in the blanks with appropriate group prepositions from those given in the box.

in spite of	according to	in front of	as a result of	owing to
due to	instead of	in the course of	on behalf of	

1. She was standing .... the mirror.
2. The whole area was waterlogged .... heavy floods.
3. The parcel was taken to a wrong address .... the postman's mistake.
4. The army lost the battle .... timely supplies of arms.
5. .... large-scale use of pesticides, our environment is being increasingly polluted.
6. .... using chemical substances in fertilisers, one needs to use environment-friendly substances for cultivation purposes.
7. You will adjust to your new school .... time.
8. I thank all of you .... the school authorities.
9. .... the rules, you must have a driving license before you can drive a car.

Let's Learn

The following is a list of some more prepositions with their combinations:

Word (adjective, noun, verb) + preposition

Preposition	Words (adjectives, nouns, verbs)
about	angry, agree, anxious, dream, happy, laugh, pleased, sorry, think
at	aim, arrive, bad, disappointed, good
for	anxious, ask, look, pay, reason, search
from	die, gain, prevent, save, suffer, protect
in	dressed, get, increase, interested, strong

Preposition	Words (adjectives, nouns, verbs)
of	accused, afraid, ashamed, assured, avail, aware, born, care, consist, details, dream, example, jealous, lack, lot, made, member, proud, remind, scared, think, widow
on	agree, congratulate, depend, get, insist, put
to	agree, attend, belong, come, complained, go, good, faithful, junior, key, kind, listen, loyal, married, nice, polite, ready, rude, sentenced, speak, talk
up	give, take, make
with	agree, angry, annoyed, argue, deal, fight, pleased, quarrelled, happy, satisfied, speak, struggle, wrong

Let's Practise

Fill in the blanks with the prepositions given in the box above and on the previous page.

1. Anita is very good .... mathematics though I'm not bad .... it! She helps me .... the difficult sums sometimes. Whenever I seek her help, she helps me. I'm strong .... English and help her .... it when she needs help. We are proud .... our friendship.
2. Our environment is facing the terrible threat .... pollution. Our teacher told us .... it in the class. All of us became very anxious .... it. How can we protect the environment .... being polluted? We agreed .... the following:
   a. We must pick .... litter if we find it lying .... the ground and throw it .... the bin.
   b. We must not play loud music .... home.
   c. We must not use vehicles which emit a lot .... smoke.
   d. We must prevent people .... throwing rubbish into the waterways.
   e. We shall tell everyone .... this so that they too can follow these measures.
   f. Everyone in our neighbourhood will be proud .... us.
   g. We must take care .... our environment.

14 Conjunctions

Let's Learn

Conjunctions are words which join together words, phrases and clauses.

Look at the following examples.

1. Breakfast *and* lunch are served to all guests.
2. Breakfast is free *but* lunch is served at a nominal cost.

In the first sentence,

- The conjunction *and* joins two nouns—*breakfast* and *lunch*.
- The conjunction and is used for addition.

In the second sentence,

- The conjunction *but* joins two independent clauses—*breakfast is free* but *lunch is served at a nominal cost.*
- The conjunction *but* is used for contrast.

The following table gives a list of conjunctions with examples.

Conjunction	Example
although	He failed to get good marks *although* he performed well in the exams.
and	He performed well in the exams *and* got very good marks.
as	I must stand by you *as* I'm your friend.
but	She had done enough preparation *but* couldn't perform well.
because	She couldn't perform well *because* she was nervous.
for	I supported him *for* I believed what he said.
if	I can come with you *if* you agree to share the fare.

Conjunction	Example
or	You can have coffee *or* tea.
otherwise	Try hard *otherwise* you'll not be able to learn this.
since	I haven't seen you *since* you left school.
still	I have watched this film five times earlier *still* I enjoy watching it.
that	I learnt *that* I must work hard.
therefore	She is very helpful; *therefore* she is admired by all her friends.
though	I came to see you *though* you didn't inform me about your arrival.
unless	You cannot understand this *unless* you pay attention.
until	You must not leave the school *until* you finish your work.
when	Call me *when* you have finished your work.
whereas	I make friends quite easily *whereas* my sister is shy .
while	Do not talk *while* the teacher is saying something.

Let's Practise

1. Underline the conjunctions in the following sentences.

a. Walk straight down until you find a brown building.
b. A bus or a taxi can take you to the airport.
c. Protect your environment, otherwise the world will come to an end soon.
d. I called out for you but you didn't reply.
e. Return your library books on time or you'll have to pay a fine.
f. Although these children are naughty, they are helpful and friendly.

g. Rani shares her lunch with John and Hema.
h. You can take one more piece of cake or a cup of ice cream.
i. I couldn't come to school yesterday because I missed the school bus.
j. We'll start from home when it is 5 p.m.

2. **Fill in the blanks with appropriate conjunctions choosing from the given options.**

a. Hurry up .... (or/and/but) the bus will leave.

b. .... (If/ Though/Whether) you miss this bus you won't be able to go to school today.

c. I always come on time .... (and/ if/ but) I have never found you ready.

d. The teacher asked us to bring some old newspapers, glue, ... (and/ but/or) a pair of scissors to class.

e. You can answer question 3 .... (or/but/if) 4.

f. You have not written to me .... (that/since/and) you left the country.

g. He is actually very mischievous .... (and/or/ but) he doesn't appear so.

h. You must regularly practise these conjunctions, ... (and/ but/ or) you'll forget them.

i. .... (Since/Although/While) he works very hard, he fails to perform well.

j. I will not know about the problem .... (if/unless/since) you inform me about it.

Let's Learn

Functions of conjunctions

Conjunctions are used to:

- add similar things to form a group.
- contrast two different elements, ideas, or things.
- logically derive something.

Types of conjunctions

Conjunction of addition

The conjunction *and* is used to join:

1. two or more things, ideas, or elements of similar type.

   Examples:

   a. Shakespeare, Milton, Shelley *and* Keats are great English poets.

   b. You *and* I can go together.

2. two sentences.

Examples:

a. Preeti wants to visit London. + b. She wants to visit Rome.
= Preeti wants to visit London *and* Rome.

c. I opened the door. + d. I found you.
= I opened the door *and* found you.

Conjunction of contrast

Conjunctions such as *but*, *although*, *though* and *still* are used to join contrasting ideas.

Look at the following examples.

1. The rabbit was fast. + 2. The tortoise was steady.
= The rabbit was fast *but* the tortoise was steady.

3. It is raining. + 4. The weather is very hot.
= It is raining; *still* the weather is very hot.
= *Though* (although) it is raining, the weather is very hot.

Conjunction of choice

Conjunctions such as *or* and *otherwise* are used to denote choice.

Look at the following examples.

1. Study well. + 2. You will fail if you don't.
= Study well *otherwise* you will fail.

3. This work can be done by you. + 4. This work can also be done by me.
= This work can be done by you *or* me.

Conjunction of reasoning and logical deduction

Conjunctions like *as*, *because*, *so* and *therefore* are used to join sentences when there is a logical connection between two arguments or ideas.

Look at the following examples.

1. I won't be able to go to school. + 2. I am unwell today.
= I won't be able to go to school today *as* I'm unwell.
= I won't be able to go to school today *because* I'm unwell.
= I'm unwell *so* I won't be able to go to school today.
= I'm unwell, *therefore* I won't be able to go to school today.

Conjunction of condition

Conjunctions such as *if* and *unless* are used to mark a condition.

Usually we use

- *if* in positive statements
- *unless* for negative statements

Look at the following examples.

1. You'll do well in the examinations. + 2. You need to study hard for that.

   = You will do well in the examinations *if* you study hard.

   = You will not do well in the examinations *unless* you study hard.

Let's Practise

1. Join the following pairs of sentences with appropriate conjunctions.

a. I want to sing. I want to dance.

....

b. Raju is naughty. He is not disobedient.

....

c. Pay attention to what your teacher says. You will not understand the lesson without it.

....

d. I went to your house twice. I was not able to meet you.

....

e. The rain must stop. The whole area will be flooded.

....

f. Mahatma Gandhi was a great national leader. He led a very simple life.

....

g. I was afraid. It was very dark outside.

....

h. We should all be together. We want to make rapid progress.

....

2. The following sentences have been made by joining two sentences with different conjunctions. Underline the conjunctions used and split each sentence into two sentences. One has been done for you.

a. One is not to be promoted to the next class until one passes the exams.

One needs to pass the exams. One cannot be promoted to the next class without that.

b. If it rains, I'll remain at home.

....

c. The new book is very useful; therefore, I'm buying it.

....

d. You must complete your homework before you watch the TV.

....

e. Do not buy the ticket for the film till I tell you.

....

f. Rathin waited for an hour near the bus stop but no one turned up.

....

g. Biju cannot join us for the practise because he is ill.

....

h. My dad is not free until he's done with his meeting.

....

3. Use the conjunctions given in the box below to join the following pairs of sentences.

since	after	and	until	if	but	because	although

a. Ryan wants to go to the party. He is very sick.

....

b. The traffic light turned green. Rohit crossed the road.

....

c. The driveway of my house was very dark. Someone broke the bulb.

....

d. You don't want to cook. We can go out to eat.

....

e. I can start laying the table. I reached early.

....

f. My brother is smart. My brother is hardworking.

....

g. Please wait here. I come back.

....

h. The food looks very yummy. We are not hungry.

....

15 Interjections

Let's Learn

Interjections are emotive words used to express strong feelings.

Interjections can be called verbal reaction signals.

There are several words in English that are sometimes used as short sentences to denote:

- the speakers' or writers' attitude
- social orientation
- emotions such as anger, dislike, disgust, fear, joy, love, and surprise.

An exclamation mark (!) is used after interjections.

Look at the following table.

Interjections with examples	Use
Alas! The great leader is no more!	to express sorrow, grief, anguish, or pain
Ah! I feel so sad.	to express sorrow, grief, anguish, or pain
Bravo! What a performance!	to express appreciation, support and encouragement
Goodbye! See you soon.	as a farewell greeting
Hello! May I help you?	as a general or introductory greeting
Hurrah! We won the inter-school competition.	to express jubilant mood, celebration and joy
Oh, no! I forgot to bring my purse.	to express disappointment
My! How tall he is!	to express surprise
Yay! I have got the tickets for the concert.	to express excitement

The following table gives a list of some more interjections with their usage:

Interjection	Use
Hi!	as an introductory greeting
Hush!	to tell someone to keep quiet
Oh!	to express surprise/sadness
Ouch!	to express physical pain
Wow!	to express admiration/appreciation

Let's Practise

Fill in the blanks using appropriate interjections choosing from the ones in the box below. More than one correct answer is possible. Remember to add the correct punctuation mark.

Ouch   Wow   Hush   My goodness   Bravo   Hey   Yay   Oh no

1. .... This shoe bites.
2. .... That was rude.
3. .... What a brilliant idea.
4. .... We're going for a picnic.
5. .... Don't share this secret with anyone.
6. .... I lost my way again.
7. .... You have been very brave.
8. .... I haven't seen a bigger cake in my life.

ART INTEGRATION

COLLABORATION AND COMMUNICATION

Activity

Think about an activity other than studies that you'd like to do with your friend/s. It could be cooking, baking, gardening, dancing, singing, or paining. Write a short dialogue between you and your friend using at least six interjections choosing from – *Hurrah! Yay!, Alas! Ah!, Wow!, Oh No!, Bingo!, Bravo! Hey!.* After you write the dialogue perform it in front of the class with one of your classmates.

Check Your Progress 3

1. Identify the highlighted adverbs in the following passage. Write the type against each adverb in the space given below.

There is sound everywhere around us. Excessive noise of mikes and amplifiers, unbearable shrill air horns of vehicles outside, awfully high sounds of fireworks during festivals are examples of terribly dangerous noise pollution. Usually, human ears can bear only a certain level of sound. Exceeding the decibel limits just once or twice may not harm our eardrum very much. However, the exposure to such appallingly deafening sounds for a prolonged period of time may cause greater harm. This alarming level of noise pollution is surely one of the causes of hearing problems in some people. Therefore, all of us must be careful about the noise levels while playing music, burning fireworks, and sounding the horns in our vehicles. Our awareness alone can remove the threat of noise pollution from the world forever.

....

....

....

....

....

....

....

....

....

2. Fill in the following blanks with appropriate prepositions selecting the correct one from the box below.

under	of	over	on	for	in	at	from
to	across	about	over	under	through		

a. Don't be late .... the meeting.

b. I'll wait for you .... the gate.

c. Could you please pass that bag .... me?

d. I heard so much .... you.

e. The rays .... the sun aid in photosynthesis

f. Rita will be .... vacation next week.

g. The snail disappeared .... the stairs.

h. I believe .... you.

i. Savitri comes .... a very humble family.

j. Go .... the road and bring some cakes from the bakery.

k. The boys jumped .... the fence and ran away.

l. The archer shot the arrow .... the hoop.

3. Join the following pairs of sentences with appropriate conjunctions.

a. She will not believe what you say. She must see it with her own eyes.

....

b. There is thick fog outside. All trains are running late.

....

c. Geeta is upset. Someone has taken her book away.

....

d. Abhinav Bindra represented India at the Olympics. He won a gold medal.

....

e. He won't come to school today. He is unwell.

....

f. Let me know. You finish the project.

....

g. I am sorry. It was my fault.

....

4. Fill in the blanks with appropriate interjections.

a. ....! I got the scholarship.

b. ....! I lost my way.

c. ....! What a fantastic film.

d. ....! I'm so sorry to hear about your accident.

e. ....! Don't share this secret with anyone.

16 The Sentence

Let's Learn

A **sentence** is a group of words that makes complete sense by itself.

Read the following sentences.

1. These books
2. I love to read these books.

In these examples, the first group of words (1.). is not complete in itself but the second group (2.). is complete in itself. The second one is called a *sentence*.

A sentence is made up of two parts.

1. **subject**—the person, place or thing that we are talking about.
2. **predicate**—the part of the sentence that tells us something about the subject.

Look at the sentence given below.

The lion	is the king of the jungle.
subject	predicate

In the given sentence, the predicate—*is the king of the jungle*—gives us important information about the subject—*the lion*.

Remember

A sentence:

- begins with a capital letter, and
- ends with a full stop (.), a question mark (?) or an exclamation mark (!).

Remember

- The *subject* is placed before the predicate.
- The *predicate* always has a finite verb. A finite verb works with the subject of a sentence to give a sense of completeness.

Let's Practise

Listen to the story of two men who were out on an adventure. Transcribe (put in written form) the audio in the given space. Circle the subject and underline the predicate.

Let's Learn

Direct and indirect object

The predicate in a sentence may have more words than only a verb. Sometimes there are words after the verb that complete the meaning of the sentence.

> The words, phrases or clauses that complete the meaning of the sentence and express the goal or result of the action of the verb are known as the **object** of the verbs.

Verbs that need objects to complete their meaning are called **transitive verbs**.

Some verbs can take two objects.

- **Direct object**—a noun or a pronoun that takes the action of a verb or the result of the action of the verb is called a direct object. This noun or pronoun is the answer if you ask 'What?' or 'Whom?' after the verb.
- **Indirect object**—verbs such as *give*, *bring*, *tell*, *take*, or *buy* take both a direct and an indirect object. An indirect object is a word or a phrase that receives the direct object.

Examples:

If a sentence has an object, it is placed after the verb. Here's the pattern of a sentence with an object:

I	love	mangoes.
subject	verb	object
S	V	O
	predicate	

She	gave	the report	to me.
subject	verb	direct object	indirect object
S	V	O	
	predicate		

She	gave	me	the report.
subject	verb	indirect object	direct object
S	V	O	
	predicate		

Let's Practise

1. Read the following sentences. Underline the direct objects in them. Circle the indirect objects, if any.

a. The teacher gave the class some advice.

b. Rohan helped Bunny while playing.

c. Please bring me a glass of water.

d. Amina carried my bag.

e. Mom bought me new shoes.

f. I met a Japanese visitor in the school today.

g. We shook hands first.

h. The postman delivered the parcel to me.

i. Granny told us many stories.

j. My doggy Bhulu follows me everywhere.

> **Remember**
> - Both direct and indirect objects are usually nouns.
> - A direct object takes the action of the predicate.
> - The indirect object is always dependent on the direct object.

2. Identify the subject and predicate in the following sentences. HEALTH LITERACY

a. This story is about the Olympic Games.

b. Athletes from around the world participate in the Olympic Games.

c. Most athletes live in the Olympic Village.

d. Athletes practise all day.

e. They compete in events.

f. The best athletes win Olympic Medals.

g. Some athletes win the Gold Medal.

h. The Gold Medal is the highest award for each sport.

i. Fans come to watch the Olympic Games.

j. Friends and families of athletes cheer for them.

k. Coaches teach athletes.

l. The Olympic Games happen every four years.

17 Types of Sentences

Let's Learn

Sentences can be of different types. Look at the following diagram.

Types of sentences

- **Declarative** = states something
  - Affirmative (positive statement): I like puppies.
  - Negative: I do not like puppies.
- **Interrogative** = asks something
  - Yes/No questions: Do you like reading books?
  - Wh-questions: Which books do you like to read?
- **Imperative** = expresses a command, request, advice and so on
  - Command: Sit down.
  - Request: Please close the window.
  - Advice: Wear a helmet while driving a motorbike.
- **Exclamatory** = expresses a strong emotion How diverse Indian culture is!

Let's Do

Rearrange the jumbled sentences given below to form a complete story. Use appropriate punctuation marks.

1. the sun did very little, but quietly shone upon the man's head and back
2. the wind went first and blew strong gusts of air, so strong that the man could barely walk against them.
3. they challenged each other to see which one could remove the coat from a man's back the quickest
4. then it was sun's turn
5. but the man clutched his coat tight against himself
6. soon a man came walking by
7. the wind blew until he was exhausted, but he could not remove the coat from the man's back.
8. the wind and the sun argued one day over which one was the stronger
9. the man became so warm that he took off his coat and headed for the nearest tree
10. the harder the wind blew the harder the man clutched his coat

Let's Learn

Declarative sentences

Sentences that make a statement are known as **declarative** or **assertive sentences**. They are of two types—**affirmative** or **positive sentences** and **negative sentences**.

Examples: 1. The children are playing in the park. *(affirmative)*
2. The children are not playing in the park. *(negative)*

Let's Practise

Rewrite the sentences following the instructions given.

1. Mithu goes shopping with her sister. (negative)

....

2. Do your friends study Italian in school? (affirmative)

....

3. Does Ali play cricket? (negative)

....

4. Doesn't your school finish at three o'clock? (affirmative)

....

5. Mrs Verma lives near our house. (negative)

....

6. Doesn't she have a beautiful dog? (affirmative)

....

7. Do you complete your homework before dinner? (affirmative)

....

8. My father teaches mathematics. (negative)

....

Let's Learn

Sentences that express a command, request, advice, order, suggestion and so on are known as **imperative sentences**.

Imperative sentences

Look at the following sentences:

1. Bring your homework tomorrow. (predicate)
2. Please give me a glass of water. (predicate)

The sentences above seem to have only a predicate and no subject. The **imperative sentences** have a hidden subject—*you.* So, the actual structure of the above sentences is:

1. (You) — subject (hidden); bring your homework tomorrow. — predicate
2. (You) — subject (hidden); Please give me a glass of water. — predicate

Let's Practise

Based on the situations given below, form responses in imperative sentences.

CRITICAL THINKING

PROBLEM SOLVING AND DECISION MAKING

1. A child is seeking an appointment from his teacher to discuss a problem. Imagine you are the teacher and answer appropriately.

2. Jaya has bought some books and made the payment. She is enquiring where to collect the items from. Imagine you are the cashier and direct her to Counter No. 5.
3. Seema is suffering from flu and her father takes her to the doctor. After the doctor prescribes medicines, her father wants to know what diet she should take. The doctor asks her to drink lots of liquids, and eat light and healthy food. Imagine you are the doctor and advise Seema accordingly.
4. Lata cannot copy what her teacher writes on the blackboard as fast as her friends. She asks her mother how to overcome this problem. The mother tells her to increase her writing speed by copying sentences from her textbook at home. Imagine you are the mother and give appropriate suggestions.

5. It is your birthday tomorrow. You invite your friend to your house. Tell her to take the road that leads to the temple and then turn right for house number 314.
6. Vani is trying to pay her taxi fare but the driver does not have change. She goes to a nearby shop and requests the shopkeeper to give her change for a hundred rupee note.
7. The class teacher commands the students to assemble near the playground on Monday for match practice.

Let's Learn

Interrogative sentences

Interrogative sentences are used to ask questions.

In **interrogative sentences**, the auxiliary verb comes first and the subject follows it. Auxiliary verbs are—*am, is, are, was, were, do, does, did, has, have, had, can, could, shall, should, will, would, may, might, must*, and *ought to*.

Yes/No question

Look at how the following declarative sentences have been changed to interrogative sentences.

1. You are eleven years old. (declarative)
   Are you eleven years old? (interrogative)
2. He can sing. (declarative)
   Can he sing? (interrogative)
3. Rohini writes stories and poems. (declarative)
   Does Rohini write stories and poems? (interrogative)

Notice that the questions above require 'yes' or 'no' for an answer. So we call these questions **yes/no** questions.

Remember

In the examples, when a declarative sentence is changed to an interrogative sentence, the position of the auxiliary verb is interchanged with the subject.

- If the main verb in a sentence is in simple present or simple past, as in Sentence 3, *do/does/did* is placed at the beginning of the sentence to make it a question.

Let's Practise

Change the following sentences into yes/no questions.

1. Drishti speaks Bengali at home.

   ....

2. Mohini loves South Indian food.

   ....

3. Ansar Ali is my friend.

   ....

4. Radha went to Hyderabad last winter.

   ....

5. Show me your homework after the class.

   ....

6. Ram and Rekha are going to Darjeeling for the holidays.

   ....

7. My brother has an electronic diary.

   ....

8. Sudha likes to draw pictures in her free time.

   ....

9. Madhu can speak Tamil.

   ....

Let's Learn

Wh- question

Questions can also be formed using *wh-* words such as *what, when, who, whose, which, where*, and *how*.

To form questions with **wh**- words (*what, when, who, whose, which, where* and *how*) the subject and the verb are interchanged, after the **wh**- word.

Examples: I am eleven years old. (declarative)
How old are you? (interrogative)

Let's Learn

Rewrite the following sentences into wh- questions.

1. Fatima is leaving today. (when)

   ....

2. Shweta was chosen for the award. (who)

   ....

3. Arjun ate the last ice cream. (what)

   ....

4. The lamb crossed the rail line. (which)

   ....

5. Vani can play the piano. (what)

   ....

6. My dad drops me at school. (who)

   ....

7. There's a doctor in Misha's house. (whose)

   ....

8. The children will play in the ground. (where)

   ....

9. We go to bed at 10 at night. (when)

   ....

Let's Learn

Exclamatory sentences

Exclamatory sentences are used to express strong feelings such as surprise, admiration, appreciation and so on.

Look at the following sentences.

1. The Taj Mahal is an exquisite monument. (declarative)

   What an exquisite monument (complement) the Taj Mahal (subject) is! (verb) (exclamatory)

2. Amitav Ghosh wrote a great book. (declarative)

   What a great book Amitav Ghosh wrote! (exclamatory)

In the above sentences, the word, *what*, is used to intensify the expression.

In sentence 1, *what* helps to express a very strong admiration for the Taj Mahal as a beautiful monument. In sentence 2, *what* expresses a strong appreciation of the book that Amitav Ghosh wrote. Sometimes in exclamatory sentences the object is placed immediately after the *wh*-word and before the subject. The exclamation mark is always used at the end of an exclamatory sentence. Exclamatory sentences can also be written without using exclamatory words. But you must use the exclamation mark.

Some other expressions used in exclamatory sentences are: *hurrah* to express joy, *alas* to express grief, *beware* to give warning, *oh dear* to express concern, *help* to express fear, *wow* to express appreciation and so on.

Let's Practise

1. Rewrite the following sentences as exclamatory sentences.

a. *Alice in Wonderland* is a fantastic storybook.

....

b. I missed the bus.

....

c. Your dress is very pretty.

....

d. Pradip can sing very well.

....

e. *The Sound of Music* is a great film.

....

f. We won the challenge.

....

g. The cliff is so steep.

....

h. Virat Kohli is a great cricketer.

....

i. Ruskin Bond is a fantastic novelist.

....

j. I forgot to complete my homework.

....

2. Read the following story and identify the types of the highlighted sentences.

Once upon a time, on a hot summer's day, a grasshopper was singing to its heart's content. It hopped and chirped all day long in his field. His neighbour was an ant. They were good friends. While the grasshopper was having a lot of fun playing, singing and dancing in the sun, the ant was working hard. It was collecting food grains and storing them in its house for the winter.

The grasshopper did not understand why the ant was working through such a lovely season and kept making fun of him. "Hey! Ant! Why don't you come outside and play with me?" he asked. The ant replied, "I cannot. I am storing food for the winter when there won't be anything to eat! Listen to me. You should do so too." The grasshopper laughed at the ant and said, "Why are you worrying now? There is plenty of food! I am not going to work now." The ant shook its head and continued its work.

Then winter came. The grasshopper could not find a single grain of food to eat. It began to starve and feel very weak. The ant saw the grasshopper looking weak and offered to share its ration. The grasshopper remembered how the hardworking ant had stored plenty of food to eat. It realized its own foolishness. "I am sorry, dear Ant," it said. "I should have listened to you. Will you forgive me for making fun of you? From now on, I will be a responsible and hardworking grasshopper."

3. **Look at the picture given below. Now that you know the four types of sentences, can you make two sentences for each type on your own?**

4. **Read the following sentences. Identify and choose the correct type of sentence from the given alternatives.**

a. The grass is green.
 i. declarative ii. interrogative iii. exclamatory

b. Think wisely before taking a decision.
 i. negative ii. imperative iii. exclamatory

c. Who is your class teacher?
 i. declarative ii. interrogative iii. exclamatory

d. My brother cannot ride a bicycle.
 i. interrogative ii. imperative iii. negative

e. My mother is a police inspector.
 i. declarative ii. imperative iii. negative

f. Wow, you did so well in your exams!
 i. imperative ii. negative iii. exclamatory

g. Do you like playing carrom?
 i. declarative ii. interrogative iii. exclamatory

h. I don't know how to swim.
 i. negative ii. interrogative iii. exclamatory

i. Please close the door.
 i. imperative ii. negative iii. exclamatory

j. Computers can be very addictive.
 i. declarative ii. interrogative iii. exclamatory

18 Phrases and Clauses

Let's Learn

Phrases

A group of words that does not make complete sense by itself is known as a **phrase**.

Examples: 1. some people in India 2. a bunch of roses

Types of phrases

Phrases

- **Noun phrase:** The phrase that has a noun or pronoun as the main word is called a noun phrase. For example, *my brother, the cat, a good student.*
- **Verb phrase:** The phrase that has a verb, or more than one verb, as the main word is called a verb phrase. For example, *can sing, will do, is going.*
- **Prepositional phrase:** The phrase that begins with a preposition is called a prepositional phrase. For example, *at home, in the room, on the table.*
- **Adjective phrase:** The phrase that describes a noun or pronoun is called an adjective phrase. It has an adjective as the main word. For example, *very poor, extremely good, too difficult.*
- **Adverbial phrase:** The phrase that has an adverb as the main word is called an adverbial phrase. For example, *very quickly, quite happily.*

Let's Practise

In the following sentences, phrases are underlined. Write the type of each phrase.

1. A captain is considered the leader of a team.

   ....

2. The paintings in the Ajanta Caves are very beautiful.

   ....

3. Characters in cartoon films are very funny.

   ....

4. My sister, Namrata, can run very fast.

   ....

5. A rolling stone gathers no moss.

   ....

6. Your sister may join you after the class.

   ....

7. The black cat chased a brown dog through the park.

   ....

8. Walking on a gravelled road is very difficult.

   ....

9. My brother was drinking hot chocolate from my cup.

   ....

10. I was disappointed to watch the new Superman film.

   ....

Let's Learn

Clauses

A clause is a group of words with a subject and a predicate. It is usually a part of a sentence.

Look at this sentence.

The sky looks blue in the morning.

In the above sentence, the group of words *the sky looks blue* has a subject (*the sky*) and a predicate (*looks blue*). So, it is a clause. A **clause** must have a verb in it. Clauses may or may not make complete sense.

Let's Practise

Identify each of the following as phrases and clauses. Write P for phrases and C for clauses.

1. I love watching films ....
2. My favourite restaurant ....
3. We are running late for school ....
4. Let us complete our work fast ....
5. Those beautiful roses ....
6. My mother and I are visiting my grandma ....
7. The new football team of my school ....
8. Mr Das took us out for a ride in his new car ....
9. Those bright yellow sunflowers ....

Let's Learn

You have already learnt the difference between a phrase and a clause. The following table shows the differences among phrases, clauses, and sentences.

Sentence	Clause	Phrase
a sentence must have a subject, a verb, and convey **a complete thought**	a clause has a subject and a verb, but may or **may not convey a complete thought**	group of words that **does not convey a complete thought**
a sentence is made up of one or more **clauses**	a clause is made up of one or more **phrases**	a phrase is made up of one or more **words**

Types of clauses

Clauses

Main clause | Subordinate clause

Main clause

Look at the following sentence.

Rani works very hard.

The above sentence has

- only one subject (*Rani*) and
- one predicate (*works very hard*).

Since the sentence has only one subject and one predicate, it can be said that the sentence has only one clause. This clause makes complete sense on its own.

A clause that makes complete sense on its own is known as the **main clause** or **independent clause**.

Dependent clause

Look at this sentence.

Rani works very hard	so that she can perform well in the examination.
clause 1	clause 2

Clause 1 in the above sentence gives complete information and may be used on its own. Therefore, it is the main clause of the sentence.

Clause 2 gives some additional information on the purpose of the action in the sentence, that is, *hard work*. It does not make complete sense and cannot be used on its own. Such clauses are called **dependent clauses** because they have to depend on the main clause to make complete sense. They are also known as **subordinate clauses** because they are less important than the main clause in the sentence.

A clause that does not make complete sense on its own is known as a **dependent** or **subordinate clause**.

Let's Practise

1. Underline the main clause and circle the dependent clause in the following sentences.

a. You can leave after you finish writing.
b. We should obey our parents who care for us the most.
c. Jatin keeps his bicycle in the bicycle stand as he wants it to be safe.
d. Fools rush in where angels fear to tread.
e. Ali will call me when his flight lands.
f. Kaushiki, who is my sister, is a great dancer.
g. Janet cannot come to school because she has fever.

h. Mary Kom, who is the only Indian woman boxer to receive an Olympic medal, is from Manipur.

i. After Rani left the room, I left too.

j. If you don't walk fast, we'll be late for the picnic.

2. Circle the dependent clauses and underline the independent clauses.

The little old town of Mayenfeld is charmingly situated. From it a footpath leads through green, well-wooded stretches to the foot of the hills which look down imposingly upon the valley. Where the footpath begins to go steeply and abruptly up the Alps, the heath, with its short grass, at once sends out its soft perfume to meet the wayfarer.

COLLABORATION AND COMMUNICATION

EXPERIENTIAL LEARNING | CRITICAL THINKING

Activity

Discuss with your partner whether the underlined parts of the following sentences are phrases or clauses. Complete the table that follows with correct information.

1. Raju placed the book inside the bookcase.
2. I already told you that I don't have time.
3. Whoever can act should meet the drama teacher.
4. The elder sister of my friend is an artist.
5. Everyone knows that a clause always has a verb.
6. Rahul has a big brown cat.
7. Riang said he will call me tomorrow.
8. A group of 50 students from an American University is visiting our school.
9. The father of the first woman Prime Minister of India is Jawaharlal Nehru.
10. Everyone knows that Radha is a good dancer.

Phrase	Clause

19 Simple Sentence

Let's Learn

A **simple sentence** is a sentence which consists of one main (independent) clause and no subordinate (dependent) clauses. It has a subject and a finite verb.

A sentence and a clause have a few points in common. To distinguish between a sentence and a clause, look at the following:

Sentence	Clause
A sentence has a complete meaning by itself.	A clause may or may not have a complete meaning by itself.
A sentence must contain at least one finite verb.	
A sentence may have more than one clause.	A clause is a part of a sentence.

Remember

A finite verb is the *main* verb in a sentence. It is a verb that has a *subject*. It shows *tense* (such as past and present) and *number* (such as singular and plural).

Look at the table below to recapitulate a few things about phrases, clauses and sentences.

Phrase	Clause	Sentence
• A phrase is a group of words without a subject and predicate. • A phrase does not make complete sense in itself.	• A clause is a group of words with a subject and a predicate which includes a finite verb. • Clauses can be of two kinds: (1) main (independent) and (2) subordinate (dependent). • A clause is considered a main (independent) clause if it can stand by itself (i.e., if it makes complete sense by itself). • A clause is called a subordinate (dependent) clause if it cannot stand by itself and makes sense only when taken along with the main clause.	A sentence consists of one or more clauses and makes complete sense in itself.

Now let us analyse the following sentences.

1. Arup Gupta *is* the son of Nipun Gupta.
2. Arup, who *is* the son of Nipun, *is* a banker.
3. Bihan Poddar, who *is Arup's* enemy, *tricked Arup's parents* parents.
4. Arup Gupta, the son of Nipun Gupta, *is* a banker.

How can we identify a simple sentence from the above list?

We just learnt that a simple sentence is made up of only one clause. Therefore, a simple sentence can have only one verb.

Let us see how many verbs are there in each of the above sentences.

- Sentence 1 has only one verb—*is*.
- Sentence 2 has two verbs—*is* and *is*.
- Sentence 3 has two verbs—*is* and *tricked*.
- Sentence 4 has only one verb—*is*.

Since sentences 1 and 4 have only one verb each, we can say that these two sentences are made of only one clause. Therefore, both sentences 1 and 4 are *simple sentences*.

Let's Practise

1. Read the following sentences. Identify the simple sentences from the following list. Write SS next to each simple sentence. Underline the verb in each simple sentence that you identify.

a. P. T. Usha can run very fast. ....

b. While doing my homework, I use a pencil. ....

c. She got up and walked out. ....

d. I love Chinese food. ....

e. My sister's name is Ranjini. ....

f. My uncle who lives in Delhi is a doctor. ....

g. You must go to school regularly. ....

h. If you go to school regularly, your performance will improve. ....

i. Sunday is my favourite day of the week. ....

j. Babli is studying very hard for her exams. ....

2. Split each sentence given below into three simple sentences. Remember to look for verbs in each sentence. Then make separate sentences using those verbs. You can also use pronouns to form the simple sentences.

a. Babur, who is the founder of the Mughal Empire in India and the father of Humayun, is a descendant of Chengiz Khan of Mongolia.

....

....

....

b. India is a big country which has many different cultures and languages and is the home of very old civilizations.

....

....

....

c. Rabindranath Tagore, who is the composer of our national anthem and who received the Nobel Prize for literature, founded the Vishva-Bharati University.

....

....

....

d. Mita doesn't like to live in Kolkata, nor does she like to live in New Delhi, although she does like to visit them.

....

....

....

e. I washed my hands before I ate lunch that my elder brother prepared.

....

....

....

f. When I was cooking, I burnt the rice but the vegetables were fine.

....

....

....

....

20 Direct and Indirect Speech

Let's Learn

Direct speech

Direct speech is the mode of narration in which a speaker's words are presented using exactly the same words and which are placed within quotation marks.

Read the sentences given against each picture.

1. Dr Sameera said, "I love to do this work."

2. "Please inform your father that I want to see him," the teacher told me.

3. Pulkit asked me, "Could you please open the door for me?"

In the sentences given on the previous page,

- the mode of narration shows the speech as directly delivered by the speaker. This mode of narration is called **direct speech**.
- the speaker is mentioned.
- what the speaker exactly said is given within quotation marks (inverted commas).
- the first word within the inverted commas begins with a capital letter.
- the verb that tells us about the **exact words of the speaker** is known as the **introducing verb** or the **reporting verb**.
  Example: Verbs such as *said*, *told* and *asked* are **introducing verbs**.
- a comma is used to separate the quoted speech and the introducing verbs.
- the comma is placed after the **introducing verbs** when it precedes the **quoted speech**.
  Example: Dr Sameera said, "I love to do this work."
- the comma is placed after the **quoted speech** when it precedes the **introducing verbs**.
  Example: "Please inform your father that I want to see him," the teacher told me.

Let's Practise

Circle the introducing verbs and underline the direct speech in the following sentences. One has been done for you.

1. They shouted, "Hurrah! We won the match."
2. Munnu asked Chunnu, "Shall we go home now?"
3. Sunita commented, "I told you about this before."
4. George declared in the class, "We received the Best School Team's award this year."
5. Mina enquired, "Will the school be open tomorrow?"
6. Ali replied, "I'm not sure."
7. Ira said, "I saw the notice on the noticeboard."
8. John requested Mirna, "Please tell me what is written there."
9. The teacher ordered the class, "Do not make any noise."
10. The postman said, "You have a post."
11. My dad asked me, "When will you be back?"
12. Mohan requested, "Please open the front window."

Let's Learn

Indirect speech

Read the sentences given below.

1. Dr Sameera expressed her love for that work.
2. Dr Sameera said that she loved to do that work.
3. The teacher asked me to inform my father that she wanted to see him.
4. Pulkit asked me whether I could open the door for him.
5. Pulkit requested me to open the door for him.

> The mode of narration in which a person reports the verbal communication between two or more people is known as **indirect speech**. Here, the meaning of the speech alone is conveyed. The actual words of the speaker are not reported.

In the above sentences,

- the mode of narration shows the speech as reported by someone. This mode of narration is called **indirect speech**.
- the quoted speech is not placed within quotation marks but made a part of the main sentence.
- since the quoted speech is no longer treated as a separate utterance, the first words in the quoted speech are not written in capital letters.
- no comma is used before the quoted speech.
- some modifications have been made while changing from direct speech to indirect speech in terms of:
  - Pronouns

    Examples: In sentence 1— *I* is changed to *he*.
    In sentence 2— *I* is changed to *she*.
    In sentence 3— *You* is changed to *I*. *Me* is changed to *him*.
  - Possessive adjective

    Example: In sentence 2— *Your* is changed to *my*.
  - Demonstratives

    Example: In sentence 1— *This* is changed to *that*.
  - Tenses

    The present tense of the quoted speech in sentences 1 and 2 is changed to past tense in the indirect speech—*love* becomes *loved*; *want* becomes *wanted*.

- A **conjunction** is used to join the quoted speech to the main sentence.

  Examples: In sentence 1— Dr Sameera said *that* she loved to do that work.

  In sentence 2— Pulkit asked me *whether* I could open the door for him.

  Sentence 2 which is an indirect question has the following changes:

  1. the auxiliary is not placed before the subject.
  2. a full stop is used in place of the question mark.

  Pulkit asked me, "Could you please open the door for me?"

  Pulkit asked me whether *I could open the door for him.*

  Pulkit asked me whether could I open the door for him. ✕

Changing the tense of the reporting verb in indirect speech

As seen in the above examples, some modifications may be necessary regarding the tense when the narration of the sentence is changed from direct speech to indirect speech.

The following table gives the rules for modification of the tense in indirect speech.

Tense–introducing verbs	Tense–quoted speech	Example
simple present	The tense of the introducing verb and the verb in the reported speech remain unchanged.	Rita *says*, "I *love* my work." (DS) simple present Rita *says* that she *loves* her work. (IS)
simple future	The tense of the introducing verb and the verb in the reported speech remain unchanged.	Rita *will say*, "I *loved* my work." simple future — simple past Rita *will say* that she *loved* her work.
present perfect	The tense of the introducing verb and the verb in the reported speech remain unchanged.	Rita *has said*, "I *love* my work." present perfect — simple present Rita *has said* that she *loves* her work.
simple past	The tense of the reported speech changes (simple present changes to simple past)	Rita *said*, "I *love* my work." simple past — simple present Rita *said* that she *loved* her work.

simple past	The tense of the reported speech changes: (present continuous changes to past continuous)	Rita *said*, "I *am enjoying* my work." simple past — pres. prog. past prog. Rita *said* that she *was enjoying* her work.
simple past	The tense of the reported speech changes: (present perfect changes to past perfect)	Rita *said*, "I *have finished* my work." simple past — pres. perfect past perfect Rita *said* that she *had finished* her work.
simple past	The tense of the reported speech changes: (simple past changes to past perfect)	Rita *said*, "I *enjoyed* my work." simple past — simple past past perfect Rita said that she *had enjoyed* her work.
simple past	Modals such as *shall*, *will*, *can*, and *may* change to *should*, *would*, *could*, and *might*.	Rita *said*, "I *shall* work." Rita said that she *would* work. Rita's father said, "She *can* work." Rita's father said that she *could* work.
simple past	Past perfect remains unchanged.	Rita's father said, "She *had finished* her work". Rita's father said that she *had finished* her work.
simple past	Simple present used to express habitual actions or universal truths remains unchanged.	Rita said, "I *work* for this company." simple present (habitual action) Rita said that she *works* for that company. Rita said, "The sun *rises* in the east." (universal truth) Rita said that the sun *rises* in the east.

Let's Practise

Change the following sentences into indirect speech.

1. The students demanded, "We want to learn music."

....

2. Disha said to me, "The bus will go to the terminus."

....

3. The Principal says, "The project is sponsored by the Education Department."

....

4. My father tells me, "I will become an artist in the future."

....

5. Ali asked Niraj, "Where have you been for so long?"

....

6. Niraj replied, "I went to visit my grandparents."

....

7. Our teacher tells us, "You must look after your parents when they are old."

....

8. Sultan said to me, "The trains are running late."

....

9. The lady at the reception said to the visitor, "How may I help you?"

....

10. The chief guest said to the gathering, "I'm so happy to be here."

....

Let's Learn

Changing the forms of pronouns

The forms of pronouns used within quotation marks in the direct speech change in the indirect speech.

Look at the following examples.

Speech	Example
direct speech indirect speech	1. Rita said, "*I* love *my* work." 2. Rita said that *she* loved *her* work.
direct speech indirect speech	3. The teacher said to the students, "Pay *your* fees by this week." 4. The teacher told the students to pay *their* fees by that week.
direct speech indirect speech	5. You said to me, "*You* have not replied to *my* letter." 6. You told me that *I* hadn't replied to *your* letter.
direct speech indirect speech	7. He said to me, "*You* can keep the book." 8. He told me that *I* could keep the book.
direct speech indirect speech	9. The teacher said to us, "*You* must carry *your* mark slips with *you*." 10. The teacher told us that *we* had to carry *our* mark slips with *us*.
direct speech indirect speech	11. I said, "*I* love *my* pet dog." 12. I said that *I* loved *my* pet dog.

- The first person singular personal pronoun, *I*, in the direct speech (sentence 1), is changed into the third person singular personal pronoun, *she*, in the indirect speech (sentence 2). This is because the subject of the reporting verb is in the third person. Similarly, the first person singular possessive adjective, *my*, is changed into the third person singular possessive adjective, *her*, in the same sentences.
- The second person possessive adjective, *your*, in the direct speech (sentence 3), is changed into the third person plural possessive adjective, *their*, in the indirect speech (sentence 4). This is again because the subject of the reporting verb is in the third person.
- In (sentence 5) the second person personal pronoun, *you*, is changed to the first person personal pronoun, *I*, in the indirect speech (sentence 6) and the first person possessive adjective, *my*, changes to the second person possessive adjective, *your*, in the indirect speech (sentence 6). Here, the subject of the reported clause in the direct speech and the speaker reporting in the indirect speech are the same.
- In sentences 7–10 also, the subject of the reported clause in the direct speech and the speaker reporting in the indirect speech are the same. Therefore, the second person pronouns change to first person.
- The first person singular personal pronoun, *I*, and the first person singular possessive adjective, *my*, (sentence 11) do not change in the indirect speech. This is because the reported clause in the indirect speech reports the speaker's own words.

- In sentences 2 and 12, the reporting verb, *said*, remains the same as in the direct speech. This is because, the reporting verb in sentences 1 and 11 does not have an object. In sentences 4, 6, 8 and 10, the reporting verb, *said*, has become *told*. This is because the reported verbs in the sentences 3, 5, 7, 9 have an object.

Let's Learn

Change the following sentences into indirect speech using appropriate pronouns.

1. Janaki said to Rumeli, "I love to ride horses."

   ....

2. The little girl looked at the mirror and said, "Wow! I'm beautiful."

   ....

3. Piyush said to Manik, "I don't want to talk to you."

   ....

4. The teacher said to Ajay, "Please bring your homework tomorrow."

   ....

5. Murugan said to Saif, "Are you feeling hungry?"

   ....

6. My mother said to me in the morning, "I'm taking a day off."

   ....

7. The students said to the teacher, "We love you very much."

   ....

8. My co-passenger in the train said to me, "Wow! What a fancy watch it is."

   ....

Let's Practise

Changing words denoting time, place and position

While we change direct speech into indirect speech we need to change the words that point to *time*, *place*, and *position of something*.

Look at the following sentences.

1. I said to my mother yesterday, "I want to take the dog home now."
2. Yesterday I told my mother that I wanted to take the dog home.

Sentence 2 refers to a direct speech taking place sometime earlier. Therefore, the word *now* is dropped. It is no longer required in the sentence that reports the past event.

3. Minal said, "My father saw an eye specialist yesterday."
4. Minal said that his father had seen an eye specialist the day before.

Sentence 4 refers to a direct speech taking place sometime earlier. Therefore, the word *yesterday* (sentence 3) is referred to as *the day before* in **indirect speech**.

The following table shows some more words denoting *time*, *place*, and *position* that change.

Direct speech	Indirect speech
ago	earlier
here	there
last	previous
next—next day/week/year	following—following day/week/year
now	then (generally omitted in *indirect speech*)
this	that
these	those
today	that day
tomorrow	the following day/the next day
tonight	that night
yesterday	the previous day/the day before

Let's Practise

Change the following sentences into indirect speech using appropriate words to denote time, place and position.

1. Soma commented, "The place looked so different ten years ago."

   ....

2. I said to the Principal, "I came to meet you last month."

   ....

3. Suman said to Nahid, "We'll meet next Monday."

....

4. I said to her, "I cannot talk to you now."

....

5. "Please place the computer on this table," said the teacher.

....

6. Deepa said to me over the phone, "I'll arrive at 10 tonight."

....

7. She informed me, "I'll pick you up tomorrow for lunch."

....

8. I said to Rita, "Deepa called me up yesterday."

....

9. An old man said to Bhanu, "Thirty years ago, I studied in this school."

....

10. The principal said to Bibhuti, "Please ask your father to meet me today."

....

Let's Learn

Changing assertive sentences into indirect speech

Some changes take place while changing the narration of assertive sentences from direct to indirect speech.

Look at the following examples.

1.	Rita said to Geeta, "I'm going home now."	direct speech
2.	Rita told Geeta that she was going home.	indirect speech
3.	Rita said, "I enjoy my work."	direct speech
4.	Rita said that she enjoyed her work.	indirect speech

- Sentences 2 and 4 are the *indirect speech* forms of sentences 1 and 3.
- The reporting verb of sentence 1, *said*, is changed into *told* in sentence 2 as the reporting verb is followed by an object, that is, Geeta.
- There is no change in the reporting verb in sentence 4 as the verb in sentence 3 does not have an object.
- The conjunction *that* is used in both sentences 2 and 4 to join the reported clause with the rest of the sentence.

Let's Practise

Change the narration of the following assertive sentences from direct speech to indirect speech.

1. The maths teacher said to Ranita, "You are so smart."

   ....

2. The School Inspector said to the Principal, "The students of your school have done very well in the last two Board examinations."

   ....

3. Alia said to Monia, "I can help you with geography practical work."

   ....

4. The principal said to us, "Mahira is your new captain."

   ....

5. My grandma said to me, "Ganguly is a great batsman."

   ....

6. Ramani said to the doctor, "I'm feeling unwell."

   ....

7. Harman said to me, "I'll bring a nice cake tomorrow."

   ....

8. George said to Ela, "My favourite colour is purple."

   ....

Let's Learn

Changing interrogative sentences into indirect speech

Some changes take place while changing interrogative sentences from direct to indirect speech.

Look at the following examples.

1.	Rita said to me, "Do you enjoy your work?"	direct speech
2.	Rita asked me whether I enjoyed my work.	indirect speech
3.	Atif said to me, "Who are you working with this summer?"	direct speech
4.	Atif enquired of me who I was working with that summer.	indirect speech

- Sentences 2 and 4 are the *indirect speech* forms of sentences 1 and 3.
- The reporting verb of sentences 1 and 3, *said* is changed into *asked* (in sentence 2) and *enquired* (in sentence 4) in the indirect speech.
- The **interrogative form** of the reported clause is made into the **assertive form** in indirect speech, that is, the auxiliary is not placed before the *subject* as in the case of interrogative sentences. The inverted positions of the subject and verb in the interrogative sentences are changed into the **regular form**—subject followed by the verb.
- A full stop is used in place of an interrogation mark at the end of the sentence, in the indirect speech.
- The conjunction *whether* is used in sentence 2, as the interrogative sentence in the reported clause of the direct speech begins with a verb.
- No conjunction is used in sentence 4, as the interrogative sentence in the reported clause of the direct speech begins with a **wh-** word.
- The tense of the verbs is changed—*enjoy* becomes *enjoyed* and *are working* becomes *was working*.
- Personal pronouns are changed.
- Words denoting time have also been changed.

Let's Practise

Change the narration of the sentences to the one given in brackets.

1. I said, "Have you left the job?" (indirect speech)

   ....

2. Mihir said to me, "When will you come back from work?" (indirect speech)

   ....

3. The teacher asked Maahi whether he ate non-vegetarian food. (direct speech)

   ....

4. I said to the publisher, "Will Dr Shahid edit the issue?" (indirect speech)

   ....

5. My friend asked the station master when the train would come. (direct speech)

   ....

6. The teacher said, "Who has removed these chairs?" (indirect speech)

   ....

7. My father asked my mother whether dinner was ready. (direct speech)

....

8. Ajit said to me, "Can I borrow your bike today?" (indirect speech)

....

Let's Learn

Changing imperative sentences into indirect speech

Some changes take place while changing the narration of imperative sentences from direct to indirect speech.

Look at the following examples.

1. Sunita said to me, "Please close the window." — direct speech
2. Sunita requested me to close the window. — indirect speech
3. The teacher said, "Do not talk while writing the test." — direct speech
4. The teacher instructed us not to talk while writing the test. — indirect speech

- Sentences 2 and 4 are the indirect speech forms of sentences 1 and 3.
- The reporting verb of sentences 1 and 3, *said* is changed into *requested* (in sentence 2) and *instructed* (in sentence 4) in the *indirect speech*.
- The finite verbs in the reported clause, *close* and *talk*, are change into the **to** + verb form. No conjunction is used.
- In sentence 4, the object, *us*, is introduced.
- Personal pronouns and words denoting time should also be changed in the *indirect* form of imperatives, if necessary.

Let's Practise

1. Change the narration of the following sentences from direct speech to indirect speech.

a. Rishav said to me, "Please help me find the way."

....

b. Our teacher said to us, "Always help the needy."

....

c. The leader said to the gathering, "Work for the progress of our country."

....

d. My father told me, "Do not waste money on unnecessary things."

....

e. He said to the stranger, "Leave the school premises at once."

....

f. The invigilator told the students, "Please hand over the scripts now."

....

g. My mother tells me, "Do not eat junk food."

....

h. The police said to the pickpocket, "Stop running."

....

i. The old man told the young boy, "Please help me with this luggage."

....

2. Two friends, Naren and Noor, are talking about a recent school trip. Read the dialogues carefully and change the narration from direct to indirect speech.

Naren: Hi! How did you like yesterday's trip to the museum?

Noor: I liked it very much.

Naren: Have you been to a museum before?

Noor: Yes. I've been to an art and craft museum before. Though it was not as big.

Naren: This was my first visit to this museum too.

Noor: I enjoyed going around different display galleries. Which one did you like the most.

Naren: I liked the gallery in which they kept a skeleton of a dinosaur. It is so big!

Noor: Yes! I couldn't believe my eyes!

Naren: I also liked the room in which they kept old handwritten manuscripts.

Noor: I loved looking at the old coins. They looked so amazing.

Naren: I wish we had more time there.

Noor: Yes. We can plan a trip with our parents soon.

21 Punctuation

Let's Do

The following passage is given without any punctuation marks. Use correct punctuation marks wherever necessary.

have you noticed how the weather is changing these days winters are not cold enough but summers are warmer than usual there is less rainfall during monsoon while untimely heavy rains are causing floods in places this severe change in the ways nature is functioning is probably a consequence of global warming global warming means a gradual rise in the earths temperature

Let's Learn

Punctuation marks

Punctuation marks help us read and understand a written passage clearly.

> Punctuation marks such as the *full stop, comma, quotation marks, capital letters,* etc., are used in the written language.

Look at the web on the next page. These are the principal punctuation marks that we use for writing.

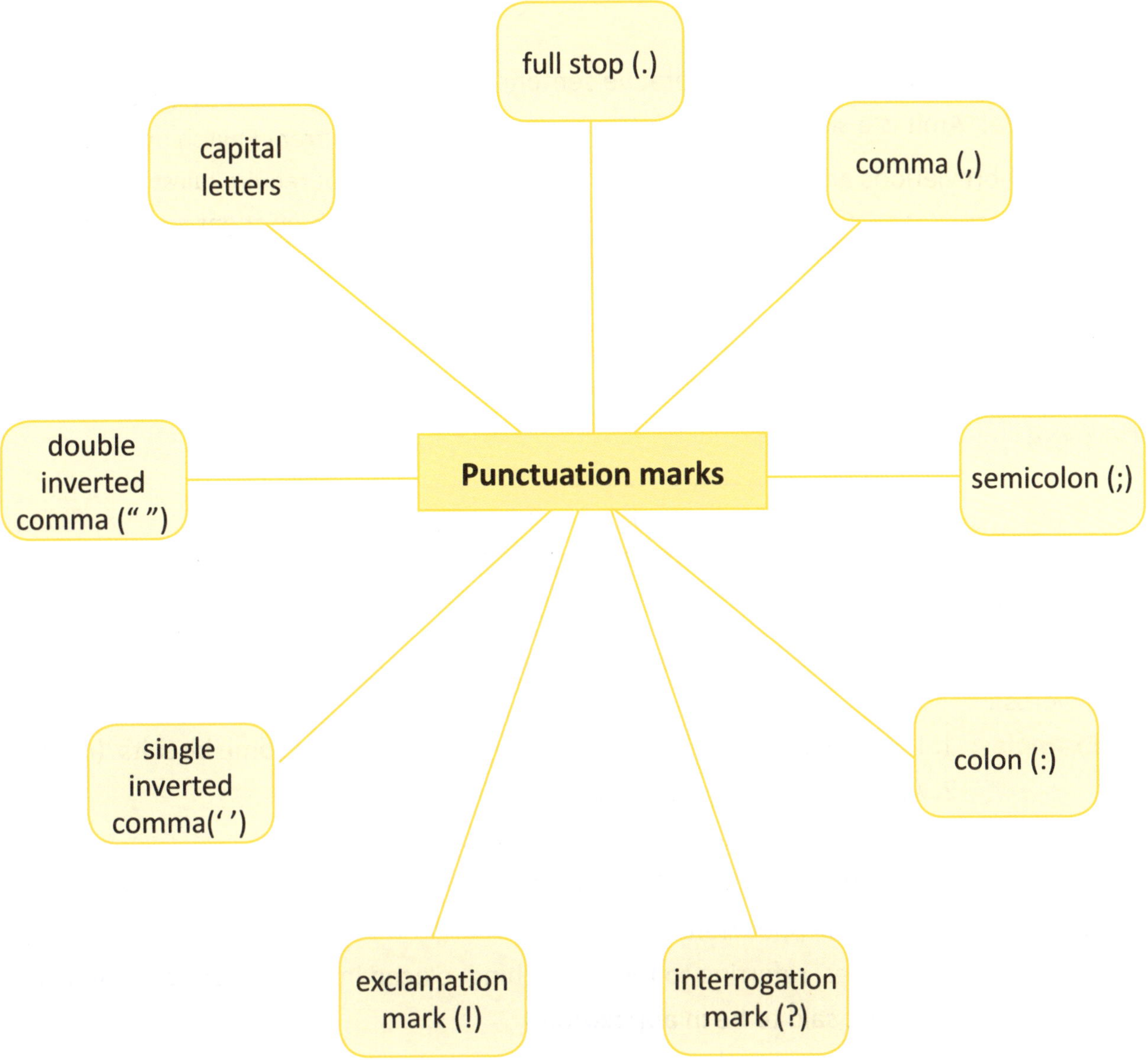

Capitalization

A sentence begins with a **capital letter**. Proper nouns also begin with capital letters.

Full stop

The **full stop** represents the longest pause.

A **full stop** is used

- at the end of an assertive or imperative sentence.
  Example: Amit is a skilled mechanic.
- after abbreviations and initials.
  Examples: M.A., S.P. Sharma

But, when the abbreviation ends with the final letter of the full word, we prefer to omit the full stops.

Examples: Mr (Mister), Dr (Doctor), St (Street and Saint)

Remember
Current English usage does not require full stops for abbreviations and initials.

Comma

The **comma** indicates the shortest pause.

A **comma** is used

- to separate three or more words of the same part of speech (nouns, verbs, adjectives, adverbs).
  Examples: 1. I want to buy some cakes, pastries, sandwiches and some biscuits. (nouns)
  2. Aziz bathed, ate, dressed and went out. (verbs)
  3. He is efficient, hard-working and sincere. (adjectives)
  4. He lifted the precious statue gently, reverently and carefully. (adverbs)
- to mark off phrases in apposition.
  (two words or phrases, referring to the same thing, placed in a sentence without any connecting word are said to be in **apposition**.)
  Example: Mahatma Gandhi, the Father of the Nation, preached non-violence.
  In the above sentence, *Mahatma Gandhi* and *the Father of the Nation* refer to the same person, so the phrase, *the Father of the Nation* is in apposition to *Mahatma Gandhi*.
- to separate words, phrases, or clauses in a sentence.
  Examples: 1. The police did not, however, succeed in punishing him.
  2. He is, after all, a very intelligent boy.
- to avoid the repetition of a verb.
  Example: Richa is an engineer and Rishi, a technician.
- to separate the subordinate clause of any kind that comes before the principal clause.
  Example: If it rains, the match will have to be cancelled.

Let's Practise

Capitalize and insert commas and full stops in the following sentences.

1. he told me that he was leaving cuttack very soon

   ....

2. i came i saw i conquered

   ....

3. pleased with the taxi driver's honesty the passenger gave him a reward

   ....

4. he is at least in my opinion a dishonest person

   ....

5. she spoke clearly methodically eloquently and persuasively

   ....

6. where there is a will there is a way

   ....

7. mithun bought two t-shirts three trousers two pairs of socks and one backpack

   ....

8. i have already visited delhi mumbai kolkata and chennai in india and new york san francisco and chicago in the united states of america

   ....

   ....

9. i dreamt of a huge brown lizard last night

   ....

10. the lizard was very big fat and spiky

    ....

    ....

    ....

11. the thief entered the bedroom through the window climbed up the stairs and examined the house

    ....

    ....

    ....

Let's Learn

Semicolon

The **semicolon** indicates a longer pause than the comma. It is usually followed by conjunctions like *and*, *but*, or *or*.

A **semicolon** is used

- to separate the clauses of a compound sentence, when they contain a comma.

  Examples: 1. The sweet, melodious music came to a close; and there was thunderous applause.

  2. Our teacher was a simple, modest, unassuming person; but we all respected him.

- to separate sentences which are closely connected in thought, where a full stop would denote a much longer break.

  Example: Reading makes a full man; conference a ready man; writing an exact man.

Colon

The **colon** indicates a much longer pause than the semicolon.

A **colon** is used

- to introduce a quotation.

  Example: Our teacher says: "Hard work is the key to success."

- to introduce a list.

  Example: These are the things we need to take with us: a torch, a flask of coffee, some biscuits, sandwiches and sweets.

- to introduce an explanation, a statement, or a proposition.

  Example: The excuse he gave was this: he had not properly understood the rules of the game.

Interrogation mark

The **interrogation mark** is used after a question.

Example: Have you completed your assignment?

The **interrogation mark** is not used after an indirect question. It is also not used after a polite request or submission.

Example: He enquired whether I had answered all the questions.

Exclamation mark

The **exclamation mark** is not used very frequently. It is used only after real exclamations.

Examples: 1. Oh dear! 2. Alas! 3. Hello! 4. What a terrific idea!

Inverted commas

Inverted commas or **quotation marks** are used to suggest direct speech, that is, to enclose the actual words of a speaker or a quotation. You can either use single or double quotation marks.

Example: "I'll see what I can do about it," she said.

Let's Practise

Punctuate the following sentences appropriately.

1. what is that father asked miranda in wonder.

   ....

2. on new year's day we went on a picnic to golconda fort.

   ....

3. i am sorry i interrupted you said the teacher please go on with your explanation

   ....

4. the sun is one of the countless stars in the sky or to put it differently most of the stars are at least as big as the sun.

   ....

   ....

5. jawaharlal nehru the first prime minister of independent india is known as chacha nehru to children india celebrates his birthday as children's day on the 14th of november every year.

....

....

6. trees help to support human life by supplying the atmosphere with oxygen essential for life moreover forest soil has a way of quickly absorbing water this helps to prevent sudden floods.

....

....

7. take care mom said to me as I was going out of the house before my examinations

....

8. the old man asked me what is the time

....

EXPERIENTIAL LEARNING

PROBLEM SOLVING AND DECISION MAKING

Activity

Find a partner. Choose one of the following passages and find out how many mistakes you can identify. Rewrite the passages correctly. Exchange with your partner and correct each other's work.

a. Did I tell you about prakash Ah yes my favourite cousin He came to visit us last weekend from jaipur We had loads of fun when he was here. on saturday we went over to Diyas house to play chess prakash is very good at chess so is Diya i thought they will be very happy to play together after they finished two rounds Prakash Diya and I went to the park. we ate two ice creams each

b. on sunday we went fishing with dad to the river prakash didnt go for fishing ever before He was exited after reaching the spot he went straight to the bank to play with the water i followed him We played for about half an hour by that time dad already prepared the fishing instruments then we tried to learn a bit about fishing dad caught a couple of trout fish and some other fish I dont know the name of we couldnt catch anything though we came back home in the evening

22 Vocabulary

Let's Learn

There are different types of words in all languages. Some are similar in meaning, some have the opposite meaning, and some sound similar.

Words with similar meanings are called **synonyms**. Words with opposite meanings are known as **antonyms**. Words that sound the same, but have different meanings are called **homophones**. (They may or may not have the same spelling.)

Synonyms

Synonyms are different words or phrases in a language that have a similar meaning.

Examples: 1. Elephants are *bigger* than mice.
2. Elephants are *larger* than mice.

The words *bigger* and *larger* are **synonyms**. Either of the two words could be used in the same sentence.

Here is a list of synonyms.

Words	Synonyms	Words	Synonyms
amazing	wonderful/incredible	calm	quiet/peaceful
angry	furious/enraged	cry	sob/weep
answer	reply/respond	cut	slash/chop
ask	question/inquire	dangerous	unsafe/risky
awful	bad/unpleasant	decide	determine/resolve
begin	start/commence	end	stop/finish
bright	shining/radiant	fast	quick/rapid

Words	Synonyms	Words	Synonyms
eager	enthusiastic/keen	great	remarkable/grand
chiefly	mainly/primarily	interesting	fascinating/appealing
falsely	untruly/dishonestly	quietly	silently/peacefully
fat	chubby/plump	scared	afraid/frightened
funny	humourous/silly	wrongly	incorrectly/inaccurately

Let's Practise

Tick the correct synonym of the underlined word in each sentence.

1. Please meet my <u>friend</u> Anish.
   a. pal ◯ b. brother ◯
   c. colleague ◯
2. The book Gita bought for me is <u>boring</u>.
   a. interesting ◯ b. bad ◯
   c. dull ◯
3. Take care and travel <u>safely</u>.
   a. securely ◯ b. quietly ◯
   c. carefully ◯
4. The new student is <u>keen</u> to learn new things.
   a. unwilling ◯ b. eager ◯
   c. indifferent ◯
5. Rina's sister is <u>scared</u> of dogs.
   a. worried ◯
   b. fascinated ◯
   c. afraid ◯

6. My dad will <u>begin</u> his new job next month.
   a. start ◯ b. end ◯
   c. comment ◯

7. I can give you some <u>amazing</u> news.

a. sad ◯ b. scary ◯

c. wonderful ◯

8. You should <u>answer</u> more clearly.

a. ask ◯ b. respond ◯

c. speak ◯

Let's Learn

Antonyms

Antonyms are words with opposite meanings.

Examples: *old—new* *tall—short* *full—empty* *open—close*

Let's Practise

Circle the correct antonym for the words given.

1. hot—cold, warm
2. foul—mean, fair
3. foolish—intelligent, silly
4. usual—extraordinary, boring
5. dead—lively, alive
6. decent—ugly, indecent
7. refuse—decline, accept
8. same—similar, different
9. harmony—symphony, discord
10. crazy—insane, sane

Let's Learn

Homophones

Homophones are different words which are pronounced in a similar way. These words may or may not have the same spellings, but have completely different meanings.

Examples: *red—read* *bawl—ball* *sweet—suite*

Let's Practise

1. Fill in the blanks with appropriate homophones from the options given.

a. .... was a boy in my class who could speak Dutch.

i. There ii. Their iii. They're

b. Jai and Mita live very close to my house. We often visit .... house.

i. there ii. their iii. they're

c. We .... to each other very often.

i. rite ii. write iii. right

d. It is not .... to tell a lie.

i. rite ii. write iii. right

e. Every religion has different .... to celebrate at birth.

i. rites ii. writes iii. rights

f. Gita wore a .... dress for her birthday.

i. blue ii. blew

g. She turned 12 yesterday. She .... the 12 candles on the cake in one breath.

i. blue ii. blew

2. Fill in the blanks by choosing the correct alternative from the pair of homophones.

a. The .... looked dashing in his armour.

i. night ii. knight

b. He said he .... where the place was.

i. knew ii. new

c. An island is a piece of land surrounded by ....

i. see ii. sea

d. Are you .... or left-handed?

i. right ii. write

e. Do you .... which one of these two answers is right?

i. know ii. no

f. Where did they .... the treasure?

i. bury ii. berry

g. Robin finished the .... chocolate!

i. whole ii. hole

h. My mother doesn't work .... anymore.

i. their ii. there

CRITICAL THINKING

COLLABORATION AND COMMUNICATION

Activity

Look at the pairs of pictures given below and write down the antonyms that the pictures represent. Then read the list of homophones. Find a partner and together write a short poem using at least three pairs of antonyms and three pairs of homophones.

List of homophones:

1. hart—heart
2. fare—fair
3. bear—bare
4. night—knight
5. eye—I
6. blew—blue
7. hear—here
8. our—hour
9. plain—plane
10. peace—piece
11. see—sea
12. I—eye

Check Your Progress 4

1. Read the passage given below and identify different types of the sentences as declarative (D), interrogative (IN), imperative (IM), and exclamatory (EX). You can number the sentences in the space given below.

Do you want to know what we did last Saturday? We went to the zoo. Our class teacher, along with some other teachers, accompanied us. My best friend Asmita didn't come with us. Oh! How I missed her that day! Our Principal had said, "Carry sufficient water and a white cap with you. Obey your teachers." We wore coloured clothes and white caps. We enjoyed our trip very much. Have you ever been to the zoo?

....

....

....

....

....

....

2. Read the following sentences from the above passage and underline the subject and circle the predicate in each sentence.

a. Do you want to know what we did last Saturday?

b. We went to the zoo.

c. Our class teacher, along with some other teachers, accompanied us.

d. My best friend Mita didn't come with us.

e. How I missed her that day!

f. Carry sufficient water and a white cap with you.

g. Obey your teachers.

h. We wore coloured clothes and white caps.

i. We enjoyed our trip very much.

3. Identify the highlighted phrases as noun phrase, prepositional phrase, verb phrase, adjective phrase or adverb phrase.

a. **All students** must wear clean uniforms to school. ....

b. My teacher **is visiting** our home. ....

c. Your dress is **very pretty**. ....

d. We **hardly ever** go out to play in the afternoon. ....

e. She will come back **in the evening**. ....

f. **My youngest cousin** is going to visit us next weekend. ....

4. Identify the phrases and clauses in the exercise below.

a. Mohit is not feeling well tonight.

b. Go to bed now.

c. My green leather jacket.

d. Five pieces of vegetable pizza.

e. I ordered five pieces of vegetable pizza.

f. A bag of crisp French fries.

Phrases	Clauses

5. Underline the main clause and circle the dependent clause in each of the following sentences.

a. We may start from home when the rain stops.

b. My brother goes to the gym every morning to keep himself fit.

c. If you don't know the meaning, please look up the word in the dictionary.

d. I'll lend you the book after I finish reading it.

e. Jai, who is my neighbour, plays badminton at the national level.

6. Form two simple sentences from each of the following sentences.

a. Sikandar, who is my best friend, sings very well.

....

b. Kolkata, which is also known as the City of Joy, is the capital of West Bengal.

....

c. Arjuna Ranatunga, who played for the Sri Lanka cricket team, is my favourite sportsperson.

....

d. Last summer, I visited Kathmandu, which is the capital of Nepal.

....

e. Mount Everest, which is the highest peak in the world, is called Sagarmatha in the Nepali language.

....

7. Change the following sentences into indirect speech.

a. Smita informed Jina, "Your father called you."

b. Jina said to Smita, "I had already spoken to him."

c. The attendant informed Rishav, "Mrs Arulmani wants to see you."

d. I told you yesterday, "It may rain tonight."

e. The teacher asked, "Can anyone help me carry these boards?"

f. My aunt said, "You are late for the party!"

g. She said, "We are going to begin the party right now."

h. The principal replied, "I've already forgiven you."

i. She said to him, "I'll never do it again."

j. The doctor told my mother, "Eat at regular intervals."

k. The coach told the player, "Keep an eye on the finish line."

l. He said to me, "They may not invite me."

m. The Secretary of the school said to my father, "The school shall serve the society."

n. We must tell Amit, "The students enjoyed your workshop very much."

o. Anjali told the principal, "I'm sorry for my misbehaviour."

8. **Punctuate the following passage. First sentence has been done for you.**

some frogs were travelling through the woods two of them fell into a deep dry well when the other frogs noticed how deep the well was they were worried about their friends they asked them not to try to jump out of it but the two frogs ignored the comments they tried to jump out of the well with all their strength the other frogs kept telling them to stop finally one of the frogs listened to what the other frogs said he stayed in the well and finally died the other frog continued his efforts at last he managed to jump out of the well

Some frogs were travelling through the woods. ....

....

....

....

....

....

....

....

9. **Look at the pairs of words in column A. Write in column B whether they are antonyms, synonyms or homophones.**

A	B
a. night, day	
b. grate, great	
c. right, correct	
d. cell, sell	
e. fair, unfair	
f. good, well	
g. shout, scream	
h. buy, bye	
i. left, right	
j. quick, slow	

Test Paper 2

Total marks = 50

1. Complete the following sentences with appropriate words given below. [6 marks]

fully because firmly sincerely next to Hush

a. Mohan's pet dog has recovered ....

b. Geeta cannot attend the wedding in Delhi .... she would be out of town.

c. Out of excitement, Rakesh held on to the trophy ....

d. Sanchit completed all the tasks ....

e. Somal's bakery is just .... the grocery shop.

f. ....! There is a meeting going on.

2. Circle the prepositions in the following passage. [5 marks]

Nawaz and Noor live with their family by the Kalighat Metro Station in Kolkata. They study in Carmel Primary School. The school building is located among beautiful, green trees on 19 Deshapriya Park Street. They walk to their school every day. Their school is situated beside Lake Market and behind Deshapriya Park. They walk along S.P. Mukherjee Road for a while and then they turn right towards Gariahat and again walk along R.B. Avenue for five minutes. Near Lake Market they again go across the road to get into Park Lane that leads to their school. It takes ten minutes to cover the distance between their house and the school. While Nawaz and Noor walk to school, all their friends come to school either by bus or on auto-rickshaws.

3. Choose the correct conjunction and fill in the blanks. [5 marks]

a. Do you want to go out for dinner .... order in some food?

i. and ii. or iii. but

b. I wanted a blue bag .... my sister bought me a red one.

i. and ii. or iii. but

c. You can't go to the library now .... it is closed on Tuesdays.

i. and ii. because iii. although

d. .... she was a talented musician, she did not become famous.

i. Because ii. Or iii. Although

e. My dog does not eat his food .... I sit with him.

i. unless ii. but iii. although

4. Fill in the blanks with the correct interjections. **[5 marks]**

a. ....! My name is Jaspal.

b. ....! That bee sting hurts so much!

c. ....! I left my umbrella on the bus.

d. ....! Our basketball team won the tournament.

e. ....! I didn't know you were coming here.

5. Match the sentences in column A with their types in column B. **[5 marks]**

Column A	**Column B**
a. My sister cannot write from left hand.	i. exclamatory
b. Please write neatly.	ii. declarative
c. Who is your English teacher?	iii. imperative
d. My grand mother is a pianist.	iv. interrogative
e. Wow, you dress looks so pretty!	v. negative

6. Identify the punctuation error and re-write the correct sentence. **[1 mark]**

"Can you pass me that rice bowl, please?", Sunil requested politely!

....

7. Write P or C to say whether the following are phrases or clauses. **[6 marks]**

a. After I took a bath	....	d. who was walking her dog	....
b. The black and white ball	....	e. The flight will land in 30 minutes	....
c. Will be singing	....	f. The sculptures on display	....

8. Choose the correct option to change the speech of the given sentences. **[4 marks]**

a. Mrs Dolma said to us, "Come over anytime for lunch."

   i. Mrs Dolma told us to come over for lunch anytime.

   ii. Mrs Dolma questioned us to come over for lunch anytime.

   iii. Mrs Dolma asked us to come over anytime for lunch.

b. "Go to your room!" scolded my mother.

   i. My mother scolded her and told me to go to my room.

   ii. My mother scolded me and told me to go to my room.

   iii. My mother scolded me and told her to go to my room.

c. Ananya asked if she could borrow my camera.

i. Ananya said to me, "Can I borrow your camera?"

ii. Ananya asked to me, "Can I borrow your camera?"

iii. Ananya questioned me, "Can I borrow your camera?"

d. Raman asked the boy what it was.

i. Raman said to the boy, "What was it?"

ii. Raman said to the boy, "What is it?"

iii. Raman asked the boy, "What was it?"

9. Punctuate the following passage correctly. [7 marks]

from the far north they heard a low wail of the wind and uncle henry and dorothy could see where the long grass bowed in waves before the coming storm there now came a sharp whistling in the air from the south and as they turned their eyes that way they saw ripples in the grass coming from that direction also suddenly uncle henry stood up

there's a cyclone coming em he called to his wife

aunt em dropped her work and came to the door one glance told her of the danger close at hand quick Dorothy she screamed run for the cellar

toto jumped out of dorothys arms and hid under the bed and the girl started to get him aunt em badly frightened threw open the trap door in the floor and climbed down the ladder dorothy caught toto at last and started to follow her aunt when she was halfway across the room there came a great shriek from the wind and the house shook then a strange thing happened

....

....

....

....

....

....

....

....

....

10. Choose the correct answers for the sentences given below. **[6 marks]**

a. Triund trek .... offers some picturesque views.

i. route ii. root

b. We must live in .... to have a civilized society.

i. discord ii. harmony

c. Miss Simran .... all our questions.

i. responded ii. answered

d. Can you please .... that tight grip on the side bar?

i. lose ii. loose

e. It is the .... before the storm.

i. peaceful ii. calm

f. The .... breeze swayed the leaves of the tree beautifully.

i. gentle ii. rough

Draw 🙂 for Yes, ☹ for No, 😐 for Some of them		To revise these concepts, go to
1. Were you able to fill in the blanks correctly?		chapters 12, 14 and 15.
2. Could you identify the prepositions?		chapter 13.
3. Could you fill in the blanks with correct conjunctions?		chapter 14.
4. Were you able to fill in the correct interjections?		chapter 15.
5. Were you able to match the sentences with their types?		chapters 16 and 17.
6. Could you identify the punctuation error in the sentence?		chapter 21.
7. Were you able to distinguish between phrases and clauses?		chapters 18 and 19.
8. Could you pick the right answer for changing the speech?		chapter 20.
9. Could you punctuate the story excerpt?		chapter 21.
10. Were you able to identify the correct synonyms, antonyms and homophones?		chapter 22.

23 Comprehension

1. Mohandas Karamchand Gandhi

KNOWLEDGE OF INDIA

CROSS-CURRICULAR CONNECT

Mohandas Karamchand Gandhi was born in Porbandar, a small coastal town in western India, on 2 October, 1869. The name of his father was Karamchand Gandhi. Karamchand Gandhi was the Diwan of Porbandar. Mohandas' mother was Putlibai, who was a deeply religious and gentle lady. Little Mohan used to be lovingly called 'Moniya' by his mother. Rabindranath Tagore, an admirer of Gandhi, fondly called him 'Mahatma' (Great Soul) for his great service to the nation. The love and admiration between the Nobel Laureate and the great Indian leader was mutual. Gandhiji used to call Tagore 'Gurudev'. Gandhiji is also known as the 'Father of the Nation'.

Mahatma Gandhi was married to Kasturba at the age of thirteen, while he was still at school. After finishing his schooling he was admitted to a college in Bhavnagar. Later he went to England to study law. He started his career in Bombay (now Mumbai) after his return from England. In 1893, he was sent to Durban in South Africa on behalf of a firm in Kathiawar to help with a case there. It was in South Africa that Gandhi discovered how badly the native Africans and Indians were treated by the British and the Dutch rulers. Once, while travelling by train, he was asked to go and sit in the van compartment by a member of the railway staff. When he refused to move out he was thrown out of the train by a constable. This incident made him decide to fight against the ill-treatment of the helpless people by the rulers. The next time he travelled by train, he was asked to sit on the footboard and again he refused. He was beaten up by the conductor for this refusal. This time he couldn't be thrown out of the train as he held on tightly to the brass rails of the train. He won the first step against violence without being violent. This incident made Gandhi become actively involved in the movement against the exploitation and ill-treatment of the people living in South Africa by the foreign rulers. His name became synonymous with protest, assertion of right and resistance through non-violence.

a. **Answer the following questions choosing the correct one from the given alternatives.**

i. When was Mahatma Gandhi born?

- ◯ 1869
- ◯ 1896
- ◯ 1893

ii. What does the name 'Mahatma' mean?

- ◯ Great poet
- ◯ Great soul
- ◯ Great mother

iii. Who gave this title to Gandhi?

- ◯ Gandhi himself
- ◯ Rabindranath Tagore
- ◯ People of South Africa

iv. Where, in India, did Gandhi go for his first college education?

- ◯ Bombay
- ◯ Bhavnagar
- ◯ England

v. Who ruled over South Africa when Gandhi went there?

- ◯ The British
- ◯ The French
- ◯ The Spanish

b. **Say whether the following statements are true (T) or false (F).**

i. Gandhi started his political movement against the foreign rule in South Africa. ....

ii. Gandhi followed non-violence because he was physically weak. ....

iii. Gandhi studied law in a college in Bhavnagar. ....

iv. Rabindranath Tagore and Mahatma Gandhi had great respect for each other. ....

v. Tagore is known as the 'Father of the Nation'. ....

c. **Complete the following sentences in your own words based on your reading of the passage:**

i. Mahatma Gandhi's mother was ...

ii. Rabindranath Tagore used to lovingly call him 'Mahatma' because ...

iii. Mahatma Gandhi was married to Kasturba when ...

iv. He went to South Africa to ...

v. Gandhi was thrown out of the train because ...

d. **Find words from the above passage that mean the following:**

i. affectionately ....

ii. kind ....

iii. fan ....

iv. found out ....

v. cruelty ....

KNOWLEDGE OF INDIA

ENVIRONMENTAL LITERACY

2. Keoladeo Ghana National Park

A park created by a Maharaja, the Keoladeo Ghana National Park, 176 km from Delhi and 55 km west of Agra and the Taj Mahal, is perhaps the only habitat created by a Maharaja. Two kilometres away from Bharatpur town, the royal family of Bharatpur developed the area in the late 19th Century.

The Maharaja constructed small dams for water conservation, diverted water from a nearby irrigation canal and soon thousands of water birds descended. The Maharaja, wanting to celebrate his success, invited dignitaries of British and Princely India to shoot waterfowl.

The sandstone in the park records the exploitation of those days. The first recorded shoot was by Lord Curzon in 1902. In 1956, the habitat shooting reserve became a sanctuary but the shooting continued until 1964. The sanctuary was upgraded to a National Park in 1981 and renamed Keoladeo Ghana.

This 29 sq. k.m. fresh water shallow swamp of Keoladeo Ghana with *kadam*, *babul* (Acacia nilotica), *ber* and *ficus* trees has 27 species of animals like *blackbuck*, *sambar*, *spotted deer*, *bluebull*, a rich aquatic vegetation, 50 species of fish, five species of amphibians, 28 species of reptiles and more than 366 species of birds (which include 32 species of birds of prey) and 379 floral species.

The painted storks, like many other birds in Bharatpur during the monsoon, are local migrants. The highlight of the park is that it is the only known wintering area of the highly endangered central population of the Siberian cranes.

Migratory birds at the park start arriving in October for wintering. That wetlands help in maintaining the freshwater flow within river systems is a known fact. In Bharatpur, the shallow aquifers of the Gangetic plain are recharged during the monsoon and from streams and wetlands in all seasons.

According to a report by Wetlands International, one-third of the world's wetlands are located in Asia.

a. **Based on your reading of the passage, complete the following sentences in your own words:**

   i. The dams for water conservation served a dual purpose for the Maharaja because ...

   ii. The purpose of the sandstone in the park is to ...

   iii. The National Park is full of ...

   iv. In winter the Keoladeo Ghana is visited by the famous ...

   v. The word in the fourth paragraph that means 'growing or living in or near water' is ...

b. **Answer the following questions.**

   i. Where is the Keoladeo Ghana National Park located?

   ii. When was this area developed?

   iii. How did the Maharaja attract the water birds?

   iv. What are the types of trees that could be found here?

   v. Write the name of three types of animals that are found here.

c. **State whether the following statements are true (T) or false (F).**

   i. The royal family of Bharatpur started this park. ....

   ii. The park is still owned by the royal family. ....

   iii. Lord Curzon never visited this park. ....

   iv. There is no fish in the waterbody of the park. ....

   v. One-third of the world's wetlands are located in Asia. ....

d. **Answer the following questions choosing the correct one from the given alternatives:**

   i. Why did the Maharaja create small dams?

   ◯ for the look ◯ for water conservation ◯ for fishing

ii. Why did the Maharaja invite the British officers and members of other royal families?

◯ to celebrate his success ◯ to imprison them ◯ to give them a treat

iii. When did Lord Curzon come to Bharatpur for hunting?

◯ in 1902 ◯ in 1956 ◯ in 1922

iv. What happened to this place in 1981?

◯ The place closed down. ◯ The place became a national park.

◯ The place was sold.

e. **Read the words given in column A. Fill in the table and write the synonyms in column B and the antonyms in column C.**

A	B	C
made		
probably		
close		
native		
several		
coming		

3. Poultry Farming

It was the hottest summer ever and there was no rain for several days. As a result, all the crops were withering away. Everyone was very worried. They knew that soon there would be no food. They didn't know how they would feed their families. Desperate to do something to sustain their families, Ravi Kumar, Majid Ali and Peter John decided to begin poultry farming. They didn't know anything about this. But they thought selling eggs and meat might be a good source of income. Hopefully there would be buyers for these and the income would be used to look after their families.

They now thought seriously about starting the business. Peter John gave the land for the farm and ₹ 1000 as his share. Majid Ali gave ₹ 3000 and Ravi Kumar provided the electrical fittings and gave ₹ 2000 as his share. Majid's wife gave some utensils for the bird feed. Ravi's father gave corrugated sheets to cover the roof of the farm. Peter's brother offered tools for building the farm. Within seven days they built their farm on the land that Peter John had given. They spent almost ₹ 4000 in setting up the farm and putting up a fence around it.

Finally, one morning they went to the market to buy chickens and a rooster. They bought ten chickens and a rooster for their farm for ₹ 1300 rupees. With the remaining ₹ 700 they bought food for the birds. At the end of the day, the three partners came back home ready to begin their new business.

a. Answer the following questions.

i. Write the names of the friends who decided to start a poultry farm.

ii. Why did they decide to start the farm?

iii. Where did they build their farm?

iv. How much money did they invest in the business altogether?

v. What did they buy in the market? How much did it cost?

b. Complete the following table using the information from the given passage.

Name	Contribution
Peter John	
Majid Ali	
	utensils
Ravi	
	corrugated sheet for the roof
Peter's brother	

c. Write the synonyms and antonyms of the following words.

i. worried ....

ii. desperate ....

iii. seriously ....

iv. income...

v. begin..

d. **Make five sentences using any five of the synonyms and antonyms given on the previous page.**

e. **How much would be the profit if the businessmen earn ₹ 8500?**

f. **Give a suitable title for the passage.**

CROSS-CURRICULAR CONNECT

4. Father William

"You are old, Father William," the young man said,
"And your hair has become very white;
And yet you incessantly stand on your head --
Do you think, at your age, it is right?"

"In my youth," Father William replied to his son,
"I feared it might injure the brain;
But, now that I'm perfectly sure I have none,
Why, I do it again and again."

"You are old," said the youth, "as I mentioned before,
And you have grown most uncommonly fat;
Yet you turned a back-somersault in at the door --
Pray what is the reason for that?"

"In my youth," said the sage, as he shook his grey locks,
"I kept all my limbs very supple
By the use of this ointment -- one shilling a box --
Allow me to sell you a couple?"

"You are old," said the youth, "and your jaws are too weak
For anything tougher than suet;
Yet you finished the goose, with the bones and the beak --
Pray, how did you manage to do it?"

"In my youth," said his father, "I took to the law,
And argued each case with my wife;
And the muscular strength, which it gave to my jaw,
Has lasted the rest of my life."

"You are old," said the youth, "one would hardly suppose
That your eye was as steady as ever;
Yet you balanced an eel on the end of your nose --
What made you so awfully clever?"

"I have answered three questions, and that is enough,"
Said his father. "Don't give yourself airs!
Do you think I can listen all day to such stuff?
Be off, or I'll kick you down stairs."

Lewis Carroll

a. Answer the following questions.

i. What was the answer of the old man when the young man asked him to stop standing on his head?

ii. What did the young man say when he saw the old man balancing an eel on his nose?

iii. How was the old man able to do a back-somersault in at the door?

iv. What did the old man eat?

v. What is the reply of the old man when the young man asked him a fourth question?

b. Complete the following vocabulary exercise following the instruction.

i. Write the synonym and antonym of *clever.* ....

ii. Write an antonym of *white.* ....

iii. Write a synonym of *steady.* ....

iv. Find the word from the poem that means 'hear'. ....

v. Find the word from the poem that means 'remained'. ....

c. Make sentences of your own with the following words from the poem.

i. father: ....

ii. stand: ....

iii. injure: ....

iv. goose: ....

v. stairs: ....

d. **Write a dialogue between the old man and the young man in simple prose for the first three questions and answer given in the poem.**

e. **Give a suitable title to the dialogue that you just wrote above.**

5. Sherlock Holmes

It was the end of September, and the equinoctial gales had set in with exceptional violence. All day the wind had screamed and the rain had beaten against the windows, so that even here in the heart of great London we were forced to look up from our routine lives to pay attention. As evening drew in, the storm grew higher and louder, and the wind cried and sobbed like a child in the chimney. Sherlock Holmes sat moodily at one side of the fireplace researching his records of crime, while I at the other was deep in one of Clark Russell's fine sea stories until the howl of the gale from outside seemed to blend with the text. My wife was on a visit to her mother's and for a few days I was a dweller once more at Baker Street.

"Why," said I, glancing at Holmes, "that was surely the bell. Who would come tonight? Some friend of yours, perhaps?"

"Except yourself I have none," he answered. "I do not encourage visitors."

"A client, then?"

"If so, it is a serious case. Nothing less would bring a man out on such a day and at such an hour. But I take it that it is more likely to be some crony of the landlady's."

Sherlock Holmes was wrong in his conjecture, however, for there came a step in the passage and a tapping at the door. He stretched out his long arm to turn the lamp away from himself and towards the vacant chair upon which a newcomer must sit.

"Come in!" said he.

The man who entered was young, well-groomed and neatly clad. The streaming umbrella and his long shining waterproof coat told of the fierce weather through which he had come. He looked about him anxiously in the glare of the lamp, and I could see that his face was pale and his eyes heavy.

"I owe you an apology," he said. "I trust that I am not intruding. I fear that I have brought some traces of the storm and rain into your snug chamber."

"Give me your coat and umbrella," said Holmes. "They may rest here on the hook and will be dry presently. You have come up from the south-west, I see."

"Yes, from Horsham."

"That clay and chalk mixture which I see upon your toecaps is quite distinctive."

"I have come for advice."

"That is easily got."

"And help."

"That is not always so easy."

"I have heard of you, Mr Holmes. I heard from Major Prendergast. He said that you could solve anything."

"He said too much.'

"That you are never beaten."

"I have been beaten four times—three times by men and once by a woman."

"But what is that compared with the number of your successes?"

"It is true that I have been generally successful. I beg that you will draw your chair up to the fire and favour me with some details as to your case."

"It is no ordinary one."

"None of those which come to me are. I am the last court of appeal."

"And yet I question, sir, whether, in all your experience, you have ever listened to a more mysterious and inexplicable chain of events than those which have happened in my own family."

"You fill me with interest," said Holmes. "Pray give us the essential facts from the commencement, and I can afterwards question you as to those details which seem to me to be most important."

The young man pulled his chair up and pushed his wet feet out towards the blaze.

(Extracted and adapted)

The Five Orange Pips by

Arthur Conan Doyle

a. Make sentences with the following words.

i. dweller ....

ii. chamber ....

iii. conjecture ....

iv. snug ....

v. inexplicable ....

b. Choose the best answer.

i. Which of the following could be the meaning of equinoctial?

- ◯ connected with an equinox
- ◯ connected to the equator
- ◯ connected to an equation
- ◯ connected to equality

ii. Which of the following could be the meaning of commencement?

- ◯ end
- ◯ beginning
- ◯ continue

c. Answer the following questions.

i. Describe the storm in 50 words.

ii. Describe the visitor.

iii. How did Holmes know where the visitor had come from?

iv. Why had the visitor come to Holmes? Can you tell what Holmes' profession is?

d. Find words from the text that have similar meanings as the following ones.

i. storm ....

ii. mix ....

iii. wail ....

iv. resident ....

v. usually ....

e. State whether the following statements are true (T) or false (F).

i. The narrator was reading a book on aviation. ....

ii. The rain had just started to fall. ....

iii. The story is set in London. ....

iv. Holmes had been beaten four times. ....

v. The visitor had come from the south-west. ....

24 Composition

1. Notice

A **notice** is a short, written public announcement made by someone to many people within or outside an organization.

Look at the following **notice** put up on the notice board:

Carmel High School, Kolkata

7 August 20xx

NOTICE

Have You Lost Your Umbrella?

Yesterday, an umbrella was found in the library. The owner of the umbrella can contact either the undersigned or Mrs Singh, the class teacher of Class VI, Section B. The umbrella can be collected during the lunch break after providing sufficient proof of ownership. The umbrella will be deposited in the office after two days, if no one claims it within that time.

Naznin Amin

Class VI Section B

In the above notice,

- the issuing authority, the date and the heading are indicated right at the top.
- the heading tells us about the content of the notice.
- the first line tells us what was found and when it was found.
- the second and third lines state what one is expected to do after reading the notice.
- the fourth line gives details regarding the final action to be taken.
- the last two lines tell us who writes the notice along with the details of the writer.

This piece of writing gives us complete and comprehensive information that we need about the lost umbrella.

The description is

- clear
- relevant
- precise

While writing a notice, the above points should be kept in mind. A notice must include information about:

- what
- description (if relevant)
- intended action
- when
- where
- the name of the writer
- the date on which the notice is posted.

Here are two more sample notices.

Notice 1:

New Era Public School, New Delhi

1 June 20xx

NOTICE

ORIENTATION PROGRAMME FOR PARENTS

The school is organizing an orientation programme for the parents of those students who have been admitted to the school during this academic year. The programme is scheduled to be held on Saturday, 4 June 20xx from 2:30 to 5:30 p.m. Parents are requested to be present for the orientation programme.

Rachel Mathews

Principal

Notice 2:

Jenkin's School, Cooch Behar

11 October 20xx

NOTICE

DRAWING COMPETITION

This notification is for students of classes I – VI of all schools in the district. Jenkens School, Cooch Behar is organizing a district level drawing competition for children in the age group of five to eleven on 12 December 20xx in the school premises. The parents of the interested participants are requested to contact the undersigned by 5 December. Participants will have to produce a copy of their birth certificate and identity card issued by the school, before the competition begins. The first three winners will be eligible to participate in the state level drawing competition to be held in the first week of March 20xx in Kolkata.

B. Ray

Art Teacher

Write notices using the following contexts. PROBLEM SOLVING AND DECISION MAKING CRITICAL THINKING

a. You lost your lunch box in school yesterday. Write a notice describing your lunch box, to be put up on the notice board of the school.

b. Your class is given charge of this month's assembly. You are the class captain. Write a class notice informing your classmates about the details of the programme.

c. Your school is organizing a cultural festival. You need to collect names of participants who will participate in the cultural programme. Write a notice asking your friends to submit their names for participation in the cultural programme.

2. Message

A **message** is a form of written communication used when verbal communication is not possible.

The purpose of a **message** is

- to communicate something very important.
- to give instructions for some urgent work.
- to provide an important explanation about something.

Both *notices* and *messages* are important modes of written communication. However, they are different in terms of form and function.

The differences between a *notice* and a *message* are:

Notice	Message
formal communication	informal communication
structured pattern	no strict structure

Look at the following telephonic conversation between Ranjit's mother and someone asking for him.

Mother: Hello!

Stranger: May I speak to Ranjit?

Mother: He's not at home. May I know who's speaking?

Stranger: This is Raju Srinivas from *Children's World Books*.

Mother: Can I take a message for him?

Stranger: Sure. Please tell him that his submission in the cartoon strip competition has been chosen as the best entry, by the panel of judges. We need to get

	in touch with him to invite him for the prize distribution function. Could you ask him to call us as soon as possible?
Mother:	Thank you very much. This is indeed good news. He'll definitely call you as soon as he's back. May I take down your contact number?
Stranger:	It is 9087667809.

Later Ranjit's mother had to go out. She leaves the following message for Ranjit.

MESSAGE

Monday, 11 May 20xx

10:30 a.m.

Ranjit,

Mr Raju Srinivas from *Children's World Books* called up at around 9:50 a.m. Your entry in their cartoon strip competition has been selected as the best entry!

Mr Srinivas needs to talk to you about the prize distribution function. Call him up immediately.

Mr Srinivas's number—9087667809. Congratulations, son!

Mom

Structure of the message

A message is very short. It contains

- only the information of immediate importance.
- the name of the person the message is meant for.
- the name of the person who writes the message.
- the date and time.

Tip A **message** need not be written in complete sentences. We can drop words such as articles, conjunctions, and finite verbs. Remember that you must not drop words that help in understanding your message.

Write down messages with the help of the following hints and contexts.

PROBLEM SOLVING AND DECISION MAKING

VALUES | COLLABORATION AND COMMUNICATION

a. You are expecting guests for dinner. Your mother has an important meeting in the office and will get back home late. She asks you to buy some vegetables and fruits. You need to go to the supermarket. One of your friends had said that she would come home in the evening to borrow a book. Leave a message for her with your maid asking her to wait for some time till you get back from the supermarket.

b. You fall ill and are not able to go to school for a week. Your teachers had told you that they would be discussing the portions for the first unit test during that week. Send a message through your brother to your best friend asking him about the dates and portions to be covered in this test. Also mention the reason for your absence.

c. The following are excerpts from two pieces of conversation. Write two messages according to the instruction given below each conversation.

i. **Sonali:** Is your brother at home, Somu?

Somu: He has just gone out. Is it urgent?

Sonali: I came to collect a book that I need very urgently for tomorrow's test. Any idea when he is expected back?

Somu: I'm not sure, actually. Do you want me to look for the book?

Sonali: You may not be able to find it—actually I don't know the title of the book. Just tell him that I came and if he can send the book to me through someone, that will be great.

Somu: I will definitely convey this to him.

Now write a message on behalf of Somu to convey the message that Sonali wants Somu's brother to know.

VALUES | CRITICAL THINKING | PROBLEM SOLVING AND DECISION MAKING

ii. **Mrs Dagar:** I was looking for the Oxford English Dictionary in the library. I need 10 copies of the book. Do you know who I should speak with?

The receptionist: You have to speak with the librarian about it.

Mrs Dagar: Can I meet her now?

The receptionist: Madam is not in her office now. Could you please leave a message for her about your need?

Now write a message for Mrs Dagar to the Librarian of her school. Mention that she came looking for the copies of the Oxford English Dictionaries for her class next week. Include in the message her question about when she should come and meet her next or how she could collect the copies of the book.

CRITICAL THINKING | PROBLEM SOLVING AND DECISION MAKING

3. Letter Writing

Letters enable us to communicate thoughts, needs, feelings and information to others when we cannot express them verbally or directly. Personal or informal letters help us to be in touch with our friends, relatives, and dear ones. Official or formal letters are written to convey official requests or suggestions as well as to serve as a record.

There was a time when letters used to be the primary mode of communication between people living far apart. In fact, letters are as important a treasure for the personal life of a person as photographs or diaries. We come to know a lot of things by reading letters written by famous people. Do you know that our first Prime Minister, Jawaharlal Nehru, used to write beautiful letters to his daughter, Indira Gandhi, from prison? Those letters are now available in the form of a book. The book is an important part of Indian literature. We still read it with a lot of interest.

However, in this age of technology we keep in touch with friends and relatives through telephones, mobile phones, and email. Though the widespread use of email and internet has eclipsed the practice of writing letters these days, sometimes we still need to write letters. Writing interesting letters is a skill that one needs to develop.

Let us first discuss personal letters.

a. Two situations, when one may write personal letters, are given below. Add as many situations as you can think of when you may need to write such letters.

VALUES

COLLABORATION AND COMMUNICATION

PROBLEM SOLVING AND DECISION MAKING

i. When we are away from home, on a holiday.

ii. When we relocate to another place and want to keep in touch with our friends or relatives.

b. Two letters are given here. Read them and say which letter is personal and which is official. Write two points to explain your answer.

Letter A

117, Sitaphalmandy Road
Hyderabad 500007
7 July 20xx

Dear Dristi,

We reached Hyderabad last Saturday by the East Coast express. I have been planning to write to you since then. But I was so busy with my new school that I could not write to you earlier. How are you? How are uncle and aunty? I miss you all.

My parents have got me enrolled into St Mary's School, near Tarnaka in Hyderabad. Yesterday was my fourth day in my new school. I have three new friends in my class. They are Raghuram, Prasad and Sanjukta. I told them about you. I also told them about my school in Kolkata.

My father is planning a trip to Kolkata during the Durga Puja holidays. I will write to you about our visit to Kolkata after father books our tickets. Please ask Pranay, Varun, Karuna to write to me.

With love,
Moira

Letter B

117, Sitaphalmandy Road

Hyderabad – 500007

1 April 20xx

The Principal

Kolkata Public School

BP Township,

Kolkata – 700091

Subject: Request for a detailed school performance report.

Dear Madam,

This is to request you to kindly send the periodic detailed report of my daughter's performance in your school for this academic year. We moved to Hyderabad last month and my daughter is now studying in St Mary's High School in Hyderabad. The principal of the school has requested me to submit a detailed report of her performance in the school she last attended. It will be of great help if you could send the report by the last week of this month.

The following are her details:

Name: Mita Sengupta

Date of Birth: 7 July 2001

Class: V

Section: A

Roll No: 5

Date of issue of the TC: 2 February 20xx

I look forward to your kind cooperation in this regard. Thank you.

Yours sincerely,

S. Sengupta

Format of a letter

A letter has a specific format. It is this format that tells us that a particular text is a letter. The tone and content of the letter tell us whether a particular letter is official or personal. A letter comprises different parts.

Let us analyse Letter A to find out the different parts in a letter.

117 Sitaphalmandy Road
Hyderabad – 500007 } A.

7 July 20xx } B.

Dear Dristi, } C.

We reached Hyderabad last Saturday by the East Coast Express. I've been planning to write to you since then. But I was so busy with my new school that I could not write to you earlier. How are you? How are uncle and aunt? I miss you all.
My parents have got me admitted to St Mary's School near Tarnaka in Hyderabad. Yesterday was my fourth day in my new school. I have three new friends in my class. They are Raghuram, Prasad, and Sanjukta. I told them about you. I also told them about my school in Kolkata.
My father is planning a trip to Kolkata during the Durga Puja holidays. I'll write to you about our visit to Kolkata after father books our tickets. Please ask other friends to write to me. } D.

With love, } E.

Moira

The different parts of the above letter are labelled using the letters of the alphabet—A, B, C, D and E. The names of these five parts are given and explained below.

A. **Sender's address**—We place the sender's address of a letter at the top left-hand corner.
B. **Date**—We write the date just below the sender's address in an informal letter. In a formal letter, we write the date between the sender's address and the receiver's address.

The formats for dates are given below.

Personal letter	Official letter
117 Sitaphalmandy Road	117 Sitaphalmandy Road
Hyderabad – 500007	Hyderabad – 500007
7 July 20xx	1 April 20xx
	The Principal
	Kolkata Public School
	BP Township
	Kolkata – 700091

C. **Salutation**—Salutation is the way in which we address the recipient of the letter. There are several modes of salutation. Salutation also depends on the nature of the letter.

A formal/official letter will use a different mode of salutation than a personal letter. For example, when we write a personal letter to a friend, we can address the friend as 'Dear Dristi', 'Dearest Jenny' or 'My dear Mohan'. But when we write an official letter to the principal of a school, we can either address her/him as 'Dear Madam/Sir' or simply 'Sir/Madam.' The latter salutation indicates a higher degree of formality and respect. Salutation is placed below the date in informal letters and just below the subject statement in formal letters. The subject statement is carried in formal letters to indicate the subject of the sentence. The subject statement is placed below the receiver's address and above the salutation.

D. **Body of the Letter**—This is the main part of the letter. Here we write what we want to communicate. The manner in which we organize the body of the letter varies depending on our relationship with the person we are writing to. The choice of words and the tone of the letter also depend on the letter-writer's relationship with the recipient of the letter. The body of an official letter will present a proposition differently than the body of a personal letter. For example, personal letters can be written on any general subject while official letters always have a specific focus. The language and tone of an official letter is very formal.

E. **Subscription**—This is the concluding part of the letter. This is written at the end of the letter, at the bottom left-hand corner, after the body. Like salutations, subscriptions can also be written in many ways. The way we end our letter depends on the type of letter that we write.

Subscriptions in formal letters are different from subscriptions in an informal or personal letter.

Here are some subscriptions:

Subscription for personal letters

i. Yours ever or Ever yours
ii. Yours lovingly' or Lovingly yours
iii. Yours affectionately or Affectionately yours
iv. Yours

Subscription for official letters

i. Yours faithfully
ii. Yours sincerely
iii. Yours obediently
iv. Yours truly
v. Sincerely

c. Some headings, salutations and subscriptions are given below. Match them appropriately to compose one personal and one official letter.

Forever yours

My dear Babu

Yours affectionately

Sameer Ali
Class VI, Section C
Bharatiya Vidya Bhavan
Chennai

George Joseph
5/1 Marredpally
Secunderabad

Babu Ram Reddy
C/o Ram Manohar Reddy
33/C/2 Street No 6
Tarnaka
Secunderabad

Sri A.K. Mondal
5/1 Lawrence Road
New Delhi - 110023

The Principal
Bharatiya Vidya Bhavan
Chennai

Yours obediently

Dear Madam

Dearest Grandfather

Write your own address

d. Some situations are given below. Select one of them and compose the body of your letter. You can choose to write either a personal letter or an official letter. COLLABORATION AND COMMUNICATION

i. You are suffering from flu. You cannot go to school for the next few days. You need to inform the principal of your school about your illness and ask for leave of absence from the school.

ii. You have received a wonderful book as your birthday gift from your grandfather who lives in New Delhi. You feel very happy that your grandfather remembered your birthday as much as he remembered how much you wanted to buy that book. You want to thank him for the gift.

iii. There are instances of road accidents due to illegal parking of autos in your locality. The entire footpath is taken over by the autos and there is no space for the pedestrians to walk on the footpath. Last week an old man was hit by a speeding motorbike while he was going to the market in the morning, walking on the road because the autos were occupying the footpath. Write a letter to the editor of a news daily about the issue so that it draws the attention of people's representatives and the municipal corporation so that the footpath could be vacated for the use of the pedestrians.

4. Diary Writing

Writing a **diary entry** is slightly different from writing a letter or a passage. We write something private and personal in the diary. We also write our opinion on something.

We usually write diaries to:

- keep a record of different events in our life.
- confide (tell something in secret).
- confess (to acknowledge having committed a wrong).
- make a resolution (a firm decision about what we are going to do).
- judge an event in our own lives.

Our diary is supposed to be read only by us and not by anyone else. Therefore, we can write about any event in our lives informally, frankly and honestly.

Read the following passages.

Passage 1—9 October 20xx Darjeeling

We reached Darjeeling yesterday evening. We are staying in the same hotel on Hill Cart Road. You know, they have a very strict schedule for everything. They serve tea, breakfast, lunch, and dinner only at the specified time. If we do not go to the dining hall on time, we have to eat out. But I enjoy my stay here. Baba and Bhai are also happy. We miss you so much.

Passage 2—8 October 20xx Wednesday, Darjeeling

I, along with Dad and Papu, reached the hotel at 5:15 in the evening. This is the first time we have come to visit a place without Mom. She had to visit her head office in

New Delhi this week. Our tickets were booked a long time ago. We wanted to cancel our tickets when we came to know that Mom could not make it. But Mom did not want us to cancel the trip. She knew that my brother and I look forward to our annual trip. She loves us so much that she wanted us to have fun. The hotel management was also not ready to refund the money. So Dad brought me and Papu to Darjeeling. Our hotel room has a very good view. We can see the Himalayas from this room. I miss my mom when I look at the mountains. All of us love to be in the hills so much. It is because of her love that we could come here and enjoy our holidays. I've made a decision—I will never disobey my mom. I'll do whatever she wants me to do. This will certainly make her feel happy.

Now let us compare the two passages.

Passage 1	Passage 2
9 October 20xx, Darjeeling—*Date* and *Place* have been mentioned. But since the date does not match with the date when the events in the description take place it must be a report.	8 October 20xx, Wednesday, Darjeeling—*Date*, *Day*, and *Place* are mentioned. The events in the description take place on the same date.
We reached Darjeeling yesterday evening.—This passage begins with a general statement which gives general information.	*I, along with Dad and Papu, reached the hotel at 5:15 in the evening.*—This passage begins with specific and detailed information.
We are staying in the same hotel on Hill Cart Road.—This sentence gives us some general description about the location of the Guest House.	*This is the first time we have come to visit a place without Mom*—This sentence tells us about some personal feeling of the writer.
You know, they have a very strict schedule for everything.—This sentence is also a general comment on the rules of the hotel.	*She had to visit her head office in New Delhi this week. Our tickets were booked a long time ago. We wanted to cancel our tickets when we came to know that mom could not make it. But Mom did not want us to cancel the trip. She knew that my brother and I look forward to our annual trip. She loves us so much that she wanted us to have fun. The hotel management were also not ready to refund the money. So Dad brought me and Papu to Darjeeling.*—These sentences give us more personal details.

Passage 1	Passage 2
They serve tea, breakfast, lunch, and dinner only at the specified time. If we do not go to the dining hall on time, we have to eat out.—These sentences also give general information.	*Our room in the hotel has a very good view. We can see the Himalayas from this room. I miss my mom when I look at the mountain.* — These sentences convey personal reflection.
But I enjoy my stay here. Baba and Bhai are also happy.—These sentences also give general information.	*All of us love to be in the hills so much. It is because of her love that we could come here and enjoy our holidays.*—These sentences give us personal information and tell us about the personal feelings.
We miss you so much.—This sentence gives personal information.	*I've made a decision—I will never disobey my mom. I'll do whatever she wants me to do. This will certainly make her feel happy.*—These sentences convey personal feelings and resolution.

By looking at the above table we can say that—

Though passage 1 appears to be a piece of personal writing, it may have been written for someone else to read. It could be a letter.

Passage 2 is written as a personal record, meant to be read only by the writer. It is a page from a girl's diary.

From the details given in the second passage, we can say that diary writing has a few characteristics.

Here are the characteristics of a diary entry. It has:

- the date, day and place
- detailed personal observation and record
- autobiographical reflection—related to a person's life
- critical evaluation of events
- personal resolution/decision
- private information
- honest opinion

Some situations are given below. Write diary entries based on them. COLLABORATION AND COMMUNICATION

a. How did you spend your weekend? Write a few lines.

b. What memories do you cherish the most? Write a few lines.

c. You come back from your school looking sad. Your mom asks you about it several times but you say nothing, probably because you think it might upset her. What really upset you? Why? Record your thoughts.

d. Your school organizes a field trip every year. This year your class visited the Science Museum. Describe the visit.

5. Story Writing

Writing a **story** involves the following steps:

- developing a story from either an outline or a topic
- giving a suitable title
- writing a moral

Given here are two stories. One is developed from the clues given in the pictures and the other from the given outline. For the first story look at the pictures on the next page and then read the story.

For the second story read the outline first and then, the story.

A. **Title:** *The Clever Rabbit*

The story

Once there lived a lion. He was the king of the jungle. He used to eat one animal every day. Everyday, the animals held a meeting to decide who would go to the king the next day. One day the elephant called all the animals and questioned them. 'Who is going to the king tomorrow?' There was no reply. Nobody wanted to die. Finally, a little rabbit said, 'I can go tomorrow.' All his friends were very sad. They said, 'Oh! No! How small and cute you are! Please don't go.' The rabbit said, 'Please let me go. I think I can solve our problem.' The next day, the little rabbit went to meet the king. The king was very hungry. He roared at the rabbit angrily. 'Why are you late?' The rabbit replied, 'My lord, as I was passing through the jungle, another lion wanted to eat me. He said that he was the new king of this jungle.' The lion shouted. 'How dare he say that! He is not the king. I am the king. Take me to him. I will teach him a lesson.' The rabbit took the lion to a nearby well. The rabbit said,

'He's hiding in the well, my lord. Look into the well.' The foolish lion peeped into the well. He saw his own reflection and thought it was another lion. The foolish lion jumped into the well and died.

Moral—Intelligence is strength.

B. **Title:** *Tit for tat*

Outline: Ashutosh Mukherjee—travelling by a train in the first class—alone in the compartment when the train started—removed his shoes, kept them under the seat—enjoyed the scenery outside—fell asleep—a stranger boarded the train at the next station—threw Ashutosh's shoes out of the window and went to sleep. Ashutosh couldn't find his shoes—understood who might have done it—he took the stranger's coat and threw it—said 'Your coat has gone to fetch my shoes when asked about the coat.

The story

One day Ashutosh Mukherjee was travelling by train. He entered the first class compartment. He was alone in the compartment. The train started. He removed his shoes and kept them under the seat.

He enjoyed watching the scenery outside. After some time, the train reached the next station. Soon Ashutosh fell asleep. A stranger boarded Ashutosh's compartment. The man was reading a book. A few moments went by and he too felt sleepy. Just before he went to sleep, he noticed Ashutosh's shoes. He threw them out of the window and went to sleep. Next day, Ashutosh woke up early in the morning. He looked below his seat for his shoes. But they were missing. He thought for a while. He knew what had happened. "The stranger must have done this!" thought Ashutosh. So he decided to teach him a lesson. He took the stranger's coat and threw it out of the window. When the stranger woke up, he looked for the coat. "Where is my coat?" he asked Ashutosh.

"Your coat has gone to fetch my shoes," Ashutosh replied with a smile.

While writing a story, remember the following format and points:

The Introduction

A lot of stories begin like this:

- Once upon a time ...
- There was a ...
- Long time ago, there lived ...

> **Tip** We generally use past tense while writing a story.

The Body

- Events must be logically connected, that is, sequence of events should be correct.
- To help readers understand and link the events, we can use connectors such as *then, now, therefore, after some time, consequently, as a result*, and so on.

The Ending

There may be a decisive conclusion, an unexpected turn of events, or an open ending to keep the reader guessing.

a. **Write stories from the outlines given below. Give a suitable title to each story and write its moral.** COLLABORATION AND COMMUNICATION CREATIVE THINKING

i. Mother Hen lives with her three children—the big bad wolf also lives close by—Mother Hen wants the children to build a house for the family—the first one builds a house of straw—the big bad wolf blows the house down—the second one makes a house of sticks—blown down by the big bad wolf—the third one builds a house of stone— the big bad wolf cannot do anything and runs away.

ii. An old man lives with his five sons—the five quarrelsome brothers fight among themselves—the old man—very sad—worried about their future—asks them to bring one stick each—sticks are brought—they are asked to break them—break them easily—the old man asks one of them to put all sticks together into a bundle—asks them to break the bundle—everyone tries—cannot break it—learn to be together so that no one can harm them.

b. **Look at the following pictures and write stories about these pictures. What do you think had happened? Give each story a nice title.** COLLABORATION AND COMMUNICATION CRITICAL THINKING CREATIVE THINKING

i.

ii.

c. Choose any two of the given topics and write stories. COLLABORATION AND COMMUNICATION CREATIVE THINKING

i. Greed is bad

ii. Honesty is the best policy

iii. Hard work always pays

iv. United we stand

6. Essay Writing

An **essay** is a piece of non-fictional writing about a particular topic. An essay carries a well thought out structured argument about the given topic.

An **essay** is a text that is used to communicate an argument, description and analysis of a given topic. Following are the steps that you can follow while writing an essay.

understanding the topic → plan and prepare → brainstorm for points → write the draft

Structure of the essay

The argument of an essay needs to be very well organized and presented through a well-planned text. An essay has an introduction, the body and the conclusion.

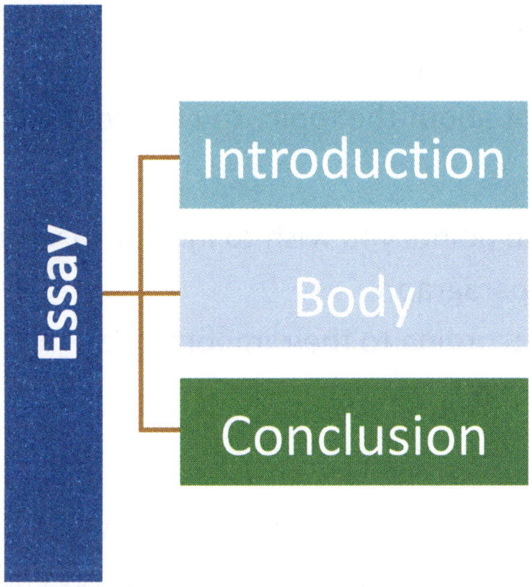

1. Introduction

   In this section, you need to write about the topic. You also need to include what you are going to say in the body of your essay. Introduction is that part of your writing through which you can capture the reader's interest. Introduction of an essay is like the headlines of a newspaper article. A good introduction will attract many readers to your argument. You can follow the following steps to make your introduction effective:

   - Begin your essay with a striking statement related to the topic. For example, if you are writing about the ancient relics of the Indian National Museum, the following sentence could be used:
     - A 5th century sandstone half-bust of Buddha from the Indian National Museum in Kolkata was stolen in 2004 shocking people.
   - Then introduce your topic to your readers in the next couple of sentences. For example, you can use the following sentences:
     - The Indian National Museum is the home for several relics from different parts of India.
     - It is one of the oldest and largest museums of the Asia-pacific region.
   - Now write your own main claim for this essay. This is called a thesis statement. For example, for the essay on The Indian National museum the following sentence could be used:

- In protecting and displaying the culture and heritage of India and her neighbours, the Indian National Museum is playing an important role since the very beginning.

2. Body

   This section can have one or many paragraphs. In this section of the essay you need to write your main argument about the topic. You can follow the following steps while writing this part:

   - It is better to write the points you wish to include in your essay before you write them as part of your paragraph.
   - Organize the points according to their importance.
   - Write the first draft.

3. Conclusion

   In this part, you summarise what you said in the body of your essay.

   For some essays, e.g. essay about your own experiences like visiting a fair or a museum, your own view can be expressed in conclusion.

Given below is a sample providing more details about how to write the introduction, body and conclusion of the essay on a specific topic.

Topic: Ancient Relics in an Indian Museum

Introduction

A 5th century sandstone half-bust of Buddha from the Indian Museum in Kolkata was stolen in 2004 shocking people. The Indian National Museum is home for several relics from different parts of India. It is one of the oldest and largest museums of the Asia-pacific region. In protecting and displaying the culture and heritage of India and her neighbours, The Indian National Museum is playing an important role since the very beginning.

Body

Founded in Kolkata in 1814, the Indian Museum is the oldest and biggest multipurpose Museum in Asia-Pacific region of the world. Initially it shared the building with the Asiatic Society at 1 Park Street. It was shifted to its current building in Jawaharlal Nehru Road later. There are two broad categories in which the collections are maintained: (1) Cultural Section and (2) Scientific Section. The Cultural Section has three subsections such as archaeology section, art section and anthropology section. The Scientific section also has three sections such as, geological section, zoology section, and botany section.

The museum is very big. It is impossible to see all the exhibits in a day. It is a better idea to plan several visits and see one or two sections properly. This museum has something for everyone. For example, if someone is interested in ancient Indian history and art, the archaeology and art sections will appear very interesting for him or her. If someone is interested in the people of India, the anthropology section is the place for his or her. If someone is interested in animals and plants, they should visit the zoology and botany sections.

The Buddha statue that was stolen was a part of the archaeology section. The statue was kept in a glass case in the Long Gallery on the ground floor. The bust came from a Buddhist monastery in Sarnath. Someone removed the glass case and stole it. Looking at the way it was stolen, people suspect that it might have been the work of an insider.

Relics like these are extremely valuable for learning about Indian history. There are several other statues preserved and displayed in the Indian National Museum. There was another incident of theft here in 1974. The thieves stole a number of antiques of the Gupta Era. However, the police were able to recover everything.

Conclusion

The archaeology section of the Indian Museum has relics from the prehistoric period. This section also has relics from other cultures including Egyptian culture. These are extremely valuable. These relics can tell us a lot of things about the period they were made. These relics are invaluable national treasures. They need to be preserved and protected with extreme care.

Now write essays on the topics given below. COLLABORATION AND COMMUNICATION | ICT

a. Deforestation and reforestation
b. School picnic
c. Dowry system in India
d. The need for communal harmony.
e. Are cartoons a good influence?
f. Games and sports
g. Care of the elderly

Common Errors

Countable and uncountable nouns

Read the following sentences.

1. I love *poetries* very much.
2. I love *poetry* very much.

The noun *poetry* is uncountable in English. As you have already learnt previously in the chapters on nouns, uncountable nouns do not have a plural form. The word *poetries* does not exist in English. Therefore, the first sentence is incorrect and the second sentence is correct.

Nouns such as *news*, *luggage*, *information*, *furniture*, *fish*, *bread* are all **uncountable** and therefore do not have plural forms nor can be used with the indefinite articles *a* and *an*.

Following are some more sentences with uncountable nouns.

1. News
   a. The news are false. [✗]
   b. The news is false. [✓]
2. Information
   a. She told me an interesting information about the coral reefs. [✗]
   b. She told me an interesting piece of information about the coral reefs. [✓]
3. Furniture
   a. My mom has ordered new furnitures for our drawing room. [✗]
   b. My mom has ordered new furniture for our drawing room. [✓]

Remember

- Only countable nouns have plural forms.
- Uncountable nouns DO NOT have any plural form.
- Uncountable nouns DO NOT take indefinite articles such as ***a*** and ***an***.
- They are used with a singular verb, i.e. verb in its base form in present tense.
- The adjectives of quantity that accompany **uncountable nouns** are *much*, *some*, *enough*, *little*, *a lot of*, etc.
- The adjectives of quantity that accompany **countable nouns** are *many*, *few* etc.

Articles

As you learnt in the chapter on articles, definite and indefinite articles are used in specific contexts.

Look at the two following sentences:

1. The Paris is the capital of the France. [✗]
2. Paris is the capital of France. [✓]

The first sentence is incorrect because the definite article *the* cannot be used with proper nouns.

Likewise, the indefinite articles *a* and *an* are also used in specific contexts. Look at the following sentences

1.	Please pass me some water.	[✓]	3.	This is a his brother.	[✗]
2.	Please pass me a water.	[✗]	4.	This is his brother.	[✓]

The first sentence is correct because water is an uncountable noun and therefore cannot be counted and hence cannot take an article that means "one".

The fourth sentence is correct. The third is wrong because the indefinite article cannot be used here. The noun *brother* already has a determiner, i.e. *his.*

Remember

- The definite article *the* cannot be used with proper names.
- The definite article *the* must be used before with superlative adjectives.
- The definite article *the* must be used when someone is talking about something specific, or one of its kind, or a unique phenomenon.

The indefinite articles *a* and *an* cannot be used

- before uncountable nouns.
- before bare adjectives – i.e. adjective not followed by a noun.
- If there is already a determiner before the noun.

Simple present or present continuous

You have learnt in your tenses chapter when to use simple present and when to use present continuous. You have learnt that we use

- simple present tense in situations such as habitual action, universal truth, general statement and planned future actions.
- present continuous to talk about an ongoing action.

Read the following sentences carefully:

1.	I'm eating my supper now.	[✓]
2.	I eat my supper now.	[✗]
3.	I'm eating my breakfast quickly every morning.	[✗]
4.	I eat my breakfast quickly every morning.	[✓]

The first sentence is correct because the sentence talks about an ongoing action and therefore the verb should be in present continuous tense.

The fourth sentence is correct because it talks about an action that happens every day. It is a habitual action and therefore the verb should be in simple present tense.

Remember

- simple present can be used to talk about habits, routines and schedules.
- present continuous can be used to talk about ongoing actions.

Prepositions

1. beside—besides

   Beside means next to.

   Example: The house is *beside* the lake.

   Besides means in addition to.

   Example: *Besides* being a good dancer, she is also a good singer.

2. since—for

   Since means from a point of time in the past.

   Example: She has been absent *since* Monday morning.

   For means a period of time.

   Example: I have been waiting here *for* two hours.

   The present perfect tense of the verb is used with these prepositions.

3. between—among

   Between is used when we refer to:

   - two persons or things

     Example: I have to choose *between* the two dresses.

   - the speaker and the person or persons being addressed

     Example: Sushant and Neha, *between* ourselves, let us admit that this discussion will serve no purpose.

   Among is used with more than two persons or things.

   Example: The British were able to conquer India because the Indian kings quarrelled *among* themselves.

4. in—into

   In refers to being inside something.

   Example: He is *in* town at the moment.

   Into refers to movement to the inside of something.

   Example: He fell *into* the river and got wet.

WORD LAB

Plurals

Regular nouns

Singular	Plural	Singular	Plural	Singular	Plural
ant	ants	egg	eggs	net	nets
bird	birds	flower	flowers	owl	owls
book	books	goat	goats	pet	pets
candle	candles	hut	huts	quilt	quilts
cow	cows	kite	kites	van	vans
drum	drums	mat	mats	wheel	wheels

Nouns ending in *s, ss, ch, sh, dge* and *x*

Singular	Plural	Singular	Plural	Singular	Plural
box	boxes	ditch	ditches	ledge	ledges
brush	brushes	fox	foxes	match	matches
bus	buses	hoax (trick)	hoaxes	mesh	meshes
church	churches	inch	inches	rich	riches
class	classes	judge	judges	stitch	stitches
dish	dishes	kiss	kisses	tax	taxes

Plurals

Regular verbs

Present	Past	Past participle	Present	Past	Past participle
act	acted	acted	burn	burned/burnt	burned/burnt
add	added	added	call	called	called
agree	agreed	agreed	care	cared	cared
argue	argued	argued	carry	carried	carried
arrive	arrived	arrived	celebrate	celebrated	celebrated
assign	assigned	assigned	challenge	challenged	challenged
bake	baked	baked	circulate	circulated	circulated
ban	banned	banned	claim	claimed	claimed
base	based	based	clear	cleared	cleared
bat	batted	batted	close	closed	closed
blast	blasted	blasted	coach	coached	coached

Present	Past	Past participle	Present	Past	Past participle
bless	blessed	blessed	collect	collected	collected
block	blocked	blocked	command	commanded	commanded
bore	bored	bored	compare	compared	compared
bowl	bowled	bowled	contribute	contributed	contributed
breathe	breathed	breathed	convince	convinced	convinced
cook	cooked	cooked	glide	glided	glided
copy	copied	copied	govern	governed	governed
count	counted	counted	grasp	grasped	grasped
cover	covered	covered	grip	gripped	gripped
create	created	created	hail	hailed	hailed
cure	cured	cured	hang	hanged	hanged
dance	danced	danced	hone	honed	honed
declare	declared	declared	hook	hooked	hooked
defend	defended	defended	hug	hugged	hugged
define	defined	defined	hunt	hunted	hunted
deprive	deprived	deprived	imagine	imagined	imagined
develop	developed	developed	imitate	imitated	imitated
dictate	dictated	dictated	import	imported	imported
die	died	died	infect	infected	infected
digest	digested	digested	injure	injured	injured
disappoint	disappointed	disappointed	intend	intended	intended
discuss	discussed	discussed	isolate	isolated	isolated
display	displayed	displayed	jot	jotted	jotted
divide	divided	divided	judge	judged	judged
dump	dumped	dumped	knead	kneaded	kneaded
dust	dusted	dusted	knit	knitted	knitted
elect	elected	elected	knock	knocked	knocked
employ	employed	employed	last	lasted	lasted
empower	empowered	empowered	light	lighted/lit	lighted/lit
embed	embedded	embedded	like	liked	liked
enact	enacted	enacted	limp	limped	limped
enhance	enhanced	enhanced	lodge	lodged	lodged
entertain	entertained	entertained	maintain	maintained	maintained
excuse	excused	excused	munch	munched	munched
exhibit	exhibited	exhibited	murmur	murmured	murmured
face	faced	faced	nag	nagged	nagged
fade	faded	faded	narrate	narrated	narrated
fail	failed	failed	obey	obeyed	obeyed
faint	fainted	fainted	observe	observed	observed
falter	faltered	faltered	obstruct	obstructed	obstructed

fit	fitted	fitted	oppress	oppressed	oppressed
flout	flouted	flouted	organize	organized	organized
follow	followed	followed	paint	painted	painted
gallop	galloped	galloped	pass	passed	passed
gape	gaped	gaped	pay	paid	paid
gear	geared	geared	perish	perished	perished
generate	generated	generated	permit	permitted	permitted
glance	glanced	glanced	pollute	polluted	polluted
prey	preyed	preyed	prepare	prepared	prepared
quarrel	quarrelled	quarrelled	preserve	preserved	preserved
quit	quitted	quitted	slip	slipped	slipped
raise	raised	raised	sob	sobbed	sobbed
reap	reaped	reaped	step	stepped	stepped
rebel	rebelled	rebelled	swell	swelled	swollen
recommend	recommended	recommended	talk	talked	talked
reject	rejected	rejected	tempt	tempted	tempted
report	reported	reported	toss	tossed	tossed
reserve	reserved	reserved	transfer	transferred	transferred
resolve	resolved	resolved	travel	travelled	travelled
respond	responded	responded	treat	treated	treated
ridicule	ridiculed	ridiculed	vacate	vacated	vacated
sacrifice	sacrificed	sacrificed	visit	visited	visited
sanction	sanctioned	sanctioned	voice	voiced	voiced
sense	sensed	sensed	wait	waited	waited
separate	separated	separated	walk	walked	walked
serve	served	served	want	wanted	wanted
shave	shaved	shaved	waste	wasted	wasted
shift	shifted	shifted	wish	wished	wished
show	showed	shown	wrap	wrapped	wrapped
sign	signed	signed	yell	yelled	yelled
skip	skipped	skipped			

Irregular verbs

Present	Past	Past participle	Present	Past	Past participle
bite	bit	bitten	fight	fought	fought
blow	blew	blown	find	found	found
break	broke	broken	fly	flew	flown
bring	brought	brought	forget	forgot	forgotten
build	built	built	forgive	forgave	forgiven
burst	burst	burst	give	gave	given

buy	bought	bought
can	could	could
catch	caught	caught
choose	chose	chosen
creep	crept	crept
cut	cut	cut
dig	dug	dug
do	did	done
draw	drew	drawn
drink	drank	drunk
drive	drove	driven
eat	ate	eaten
fall	fell	fallen
feed	fed	fed
feel	felt	felt
arise	arose	arisen
awake	awoke	awoken
be/is	was	been
am	was	been
are	were	been
begin	began	begun
bid	bade	bidden
sell	sold	sold
send	sent	sent
set	set	set
shake	shook	shaken
shine	shone	shone
shoot	shot	shot
show	showed	shown
shrink	shrank	shrunk
shut	shut	shut
sing	sang	sung
sink	sank	sunk
sit	sat	sat
sleep	slept	slept
sow	sowed	sown
read	read (pronounced as red)	read (pronounced as red)
ride	rode	ridden
rise	rose	risen
ring	rang	rung

go	went	gone
grow	grew	grown
have	had	had
hide	hid	hidden
hit	hit	hit
hold	held	held
hurt	hurt	hurt
keep	kept	kept
know	knew	known
lay	laid	laid
lead	led	led
learn	learnt	learnt
lend	lent	lent
let	let	let
lose	lost	lost
make	made	made
mean	meant	meant
meet	met	met
put	put	put
run	ran	run
see	saw	seen
seek	sought	sought
speak	spoke	spoken
spread	spread	spread
steal	stole	stolen
stick	stuck	stuck
strike	struck	struck
swear	swore	sworn
swim	swam	swum
take	took	taken
teach	taught	taught
tear	tore	torn
tell	told	told
think	thought	thought
throw	threw	thrown
thrust	thrust	thrust
wake	woke	woken
wear	wore	worn
weave	wove	woven
weep	wept	wept
write	wrote	written

Antonyms

Words	Antonyms	Words	Antonyms
liquid	solid	left	right
bad	good	excellent	lousy
up	down	friend	enemy
right	wrong	hard	soft
large/big	small	holy	unholy
happy	sad	polite	rude
light	heavy	clean	dirty
gentle	rough	ugly	beautiful
wet	dry	win	lose

Homophones

Homophones	Meaning	Homophones	Meaning
aid (V) aide (N)	to assist an assistant	blew (V) blue (N)	past tense of 'blow' a colour
air (N) heir (N)	the mixture of gases we breathe one who will inherit	broach (V) brooch (N)	to raise a subject an ornament fastened to clothes
ail (V) ale (N)	to be sick a type of beer	bold (Adj) bowled (V)	brave knocked over
altar (N) alter (V)	a holy structure found in religious places to change	cast (V) caste (N)	to throw social class
ascent (N) assent (N)	the act of climbing up agreement	born (V) borne (V)	came into being past participle of 'bear'
bard (N) barred (V)	a poet enclosed with bars or poles	cereal (N) serial (Adj)	grains in sequence
bare (Adj) bear (N)	naked a wild animal	peace (N) piece (N)	a situation without violence a single item
eye (N) I (N)	the organ of sight oneself	cite (V) sight (N) site (N)	refer to vision a place or setting
board (N) bored (Adj)	a plank not interested	doe (N) dough (N)	a female deer a mixture of flour and water
boy (N) bouy (N)	a young male anchored float	higher (Adj) hire (V)	comparative form of 'high' to employ
berth (N) birth (N)	a place to sleep in on a ship or train the process of being born	fair (Adj) fare (N)	just money paid for travel
bread (N) bred (V)	a loaf past tense of 'breed'	cue (N) queue (N)	a signal a waiting line

find (V) fined (V)	to locate to have to pay as punishment	foul (Adj) fowl (N)	grossly offensive or bad domestic hen or cock
flea (N) flee (V)	an insect to run away	hear (V) here (Adj)	to listen at this location
incite (V) insight (N)	to provoke understanding	buy (V) by (Prep) bye (N)	to purchase near word used to bid farewell
beach (N) beech (N)	an area of sand along the sea a type of tree	meat (N) meet (V)	flesh of animals to come together and talk
bard (N) barred (V)	a poet enclosed with bars or poles	hart (N) heart (N)	a deer organ in the chest that pumps blood
band (N) banned (V)	a group forbidden	one (Det) won (V)	the first number was victorious
bean (N) been (V)	a legume past tense of 'be'	heal (V) heel (N)	to cure a disease the back part of the foot
beat (V) beet (N)	to hit an edible red root	plain (Adj) plane (N)	not fanciful a surface
be (V) bee (V)	to exist an insect	lead (N) led (V)	a heavy metal guided
boar (N) bore (N)	a wild pig someone or something not interesting	hour (N) our (Det)	a period of sixty minutes possessed by us
bell (N) belle (N)	an object that makes a ringing sound a beautiful woman	mail (N) male (Adj)	letter one who belongs to the masculine gender
him (pronoun) hymn (N)	third person singular, masculine a religious song	scent (N) sent (V)	aroma dispatched
hole (N) whole (Adj)	a round opening full or complete	knot (N) not (Adv)	a fastening in a cord used to show negation
feat (N) feet (N)	an accomplishment the part below the ankle	knight (N) night (N)	a chivalrous man the period of darkness between one day and another
flew (V) flu (N)	past tense of 'fly' short form of influenza	loan (N) lone (Adj)	something borrowed without others
know (V) no (Adv/Det)	to be aware of used to show negation	cell (N) sell (V)	a small room to exchange something for money
groan (N) grown (Adj)	a long, deep sound of anger, pain, or pleasure become big		